Understanding and Using PC-Write
Version 2.71

Victor P. Maiorana

Queensborough Community College

West Publishing Company
St. Paul   New York   Los Angeles   San Francisco

Copyeditor: Beth Bulger
Cover Design: Bob Anderson, Computer Arts, Inc.

Screens, Quick Reference Card material, and Appendix G are reprinted with the permission of Quicksoft.

Appendix B is based on material from <u>How to Learn and Study in College</u> (Maiorana, 1980, pp. 132, 173-177), and is reprinted with the permission of Prentice-Hall.

Library of Congress Cataloging-in-Publication Data

Maiorana, Victor P.
   Understanding and using PC-Write.

   (The Microcomputing series)
   Includes index.
   1. PC-Write (Computer program) 2. Word processing
I. Title. II. Series.
Z52.5.P35M34 1988   652'.5   87-24265
ISBN 0-314-30119-4

CONTENTS

UNIT 3   LOADING AND EDITING A DOCUMENT   31

UNIT 4   CREATING A NEW DOCUMENT   57

TABLES

FIGURES

GUIDED ACTIVITIES

UNIT 3 LOADING AND EDITING A DOCUMENT

UNIT 4 CREATING A NEW DOCUMENT

UNIT 5 SAVING A PRINTING A DOCUMENT

UNIT 6 TEXT AND PAGE FORMATTING

UNIT 7 COPYING AND MOVING TEXT

PUBLISHER'S NOTE

This book is part of THE MICROCOMPUTING SERIES. We are proud to announce that this unique series is now entering its third year, and currently includes four different types of books:

1. A core concepts book, now in its second edition, teaches basic hardware and software applications concepts. This text is titled UNDERSTANDING AND USING MICROCOMPUTERS.

2. A series of introductory level, hands-on workbooks for a wide variety of specific software packages. These provide both self-paced tutorials and complete reference guides. Each book's title begins with UNDERSTANDING AND USING . . . .

3. Several larger volumes combine DOS with three popular software packages. Two of these volumes are called UNDERSTANDING AND USING APPLICATION SOFTWARE, while the third is titled UNDERSTANDING AND USING SHAREWARE APPLICATION SOFTWARE. These versions condense components of the individual workbooks while increasing the coverage of DOS and the integration of different application packages.

4. An advanced level of hands-on workbooks with a strong project/systems orientation. These titles all begin with DEVELOPING AND USING . . . .

Our goal has always been to provide you with maximum flexibility in meeting the changing needs of your courses through this "mix and match" approach. We remain committed to offering the widest variety of current softwear packages.

We now offer these books in THE MICROCOMPUTING SERIES:

Understanding and Using Microcomputers, second edition   by Steven M. Zimmerman and Leo M. Conrad

OPERATING SYSTEMS

Understanding and Using MS-DOS/PC DOS:
The First Steps
    by Laura B. Ruff and Mary K. Weitzer

Understanding and Using MS-DOS/PC DOS:
A Complete Guide
    by Cody T. Copeland and Jonathan P. Bacon

PROGRAMMING LANGUAGES

Understanding and Using Microsoft BASIC/IBM-PC BASIC
    by Mary L. Howard

WORD PROCESSORS

Understanding and Using Displaywrite 3 and Displaywrite 4
    by Patsy H. Lund and Barbara A. Hayden

Understanding and Using Microsoft Word
    by Jonathan P. Bacon

Understanding and Using MultiMate
    by Mary K.Weitzer and Laura B. Ruff

Understanding and Using PC-Write
    by Victor P. Maiorana

Understanding and Using pfs:WRITE
    by Mary K. Weitzer and Laura B. Ruff

Understanding and Using WordPerfect
    by Patsy H. Lund, Barbara A. Hayden,
    and Sharon S. Larsen

Understanding and Using WordStar
    by Steven C. Ross

Understanding and Using WordStar 4.0
    by Patsy H. Lund and Barbara A. Hayden

SPREADSHEET PACKAGES

Understanding and Using ExpressCalc (Including PC-CALC)
    by Victor P. Maiorana and Arthur A. Strunk

Understanding and Using Lotus 1-2-3
    by Steven C. Ross

Understanding and Using Lotus 1-2-3 Release 2
    by Steven C. Ross

Understanding and Using SuperCalc 3
    by Steven C. Ross and Judy A. Reinders

Understanding and Using Super Calc 4
    by Judy A. Reinders and Steven C. Ross

DATABASE PACKAGES

Understanding and Using dBASE III (Including dBASE II)
    by Steven C. Ross

Understanding and Using dBASE III PLUS
    by Steven C. Ross

Understanding and Using PC-FILE III
    by Victor P. Maiorana and Arthur A. Strunk

Understanding and Using pfs:FILE/REPORT
    by Laura B. Ruff and Mary K. Weitzer

Understanding and Using R:BASE 5000
(including R:BASE System V)
    by Karen L. Watterson

INTEGRATED SOFTWARE

Understanding and Using AppleWorks
    by Frank Short

Understanding and Using Educate-Ability
    by Victor P. Maiorana and Arthur A. Strunk

Understanding and Using FRAMEWORK
    by Karen L. Watterson

Developing and Using Office Applications with AppleWorks
    by M. S. Varnon

Understanding and Using Symphony
    by Enzo V. Allegretti

COMBINATION VOLUMES

Understanding and Using Application Software, Volume 1:
DOS, WordStar 4.0, Lotus 1-2-3 Release 2, and dBASE III Plus
    by Patsy H. Lund, Barbara A. Hayden, and Steven C. Ross

Understanding and Using Application Software, Volume 2:
DOS, WordPerfect, Lotus 1-2-3 Release 2, and dBASE III Plus
    by Patsy H. Lund, Barbara A. Hayden, and Steven C. Ross

Understanding and Using SHAREWARE Application Software:
DOS, PC-Write, ExpressCalc, and PC-FILE
    by Victor P. Maiorana and Arthur A. Strunk

ADVANCED BOOKS

Developing and Using Advanced Lotus 1-2-3 Applications
    by Steven C. Ross

Developing and Using Decision Support Applications
    by Steven C. Ross, Richard J. Penlesky, and Lloyd D. Doney

Developing and Using Microcomputer Business Systems
    by Kathryn W. Huff

We are delighted by the popularity of THE MICROCOMPUTING SERIES. We appreciate your support, and look forward to your suggestions and comments. Please write to us at this address:

West Publishing Company
College Division
50 West Kellogg Blvd.
P.O. Box 64526
St. Paul, MN 55164

ABOUT THE AUTHOR

Victor P. Maiorana holds a B.S. degree in electrical engineering from Brooklyn Polytechnic Institute, an M.B.A. from Adelphi University, and a Ph.D. from New York University. The author of several books, including the popular *How To Learn and Study In College*, Dr. Maiorana received the 1985 New York University Paul S. Lomax award for scholarship and leadership in business education. He has taught at both two-year and four-year colleges, and was responsible for the introduction of microcomputers and application software into the undergraduate and graduate business curriculum at Dowling College. Dr. Maiorana is a faculty member in the business department at Queensborough Community College.

PREFACE

In no operation can the disposition of a crew be discovered better than in getting under weigh.

Dana, Two Years Before the Mast

The widespread use of microcomputers brings with it questions such as these: "Is learning to write still important?" and "Will the written word disappear?"

Despite the advent of the microcomputer, the chances are excellent that the need to write will persist. Writing has been, continues to be, and will probably always be an essential part of social, artistic, political, and business affairs.

Words on a page stay fixed. They provide a basis for reaching understanding and agreement. The words can be changed to reflect the agreement. This is a critical and widely used process. Words on a page promote a unique opportunity for study and analysis; they promote the dissemination of facts and ideas and allow the imagination to roam free. Possessing these and other important and vital functions, the skill of writing is not likely to fall into disuse.

WHY THIS BOOK?

Since writing is important, tools such as computers and computer programs should be used to the best possible advantage to aid the writing process. This book addresses two such tools: the International Business Machines Personal Computer (IBM PC), and a program which instructs the computer: the PC-Write word processor by Quicksoft. PC-Write is a shareware product of the Quicksoft Company, 219 First N. #224, Seattle, Washington, 98109. Among other things, shareware means that copies can be made available to users free of charge (see the appendix for additional discussion of the shareware concept).

This book should do at least these things for you:

> Help you understand and use fundamental, intermediate, and advanced operations of a word processing computer program called PC-Write. PC-Write will help turn what you write into a clear, presentable, professional-quality document.

Provide you with a sense of accomplishment, as you see your thoughts turned into a printed document.

Improve your writing skills.

Unlike many word processing software manuals, this text allows both the student and the instructor to operate within a sound educational framework. Each unit includes the following features:

Learning Objectives: The knowledge and skills to be addressed in the unit.

Subject Matter Experiences: the groundwork necessary for gaining confidence and mastery is provided by exploring existing word processing documents before original documents are created.

Start-to-Finish General Procedures: the detailed sequence of steps necessary to the understanding and use of specific word processing functions.

Guided Activities: hands-on skill-building illustrations of the operations discussed in the unit.

Review Questions: questions designed to test the level of knowledge and understanding of the material presented. Space is provided for recording answers.

Documentation Research: exercises that require the use of the software publisher's documentation to enlarge your knowledge of commands functions discussed in the unit.

Additional features of *Understanding and Using PC-Write* are as follows:

Application Exercises: Nine exercises spread throughout the book which are designed to be more challenging than the guided activities.

Getting Started on Your Microcomputer: an appendix that provides a broad introduction to microcomputer systems and the IBM PC disk operating system.

The Writing Plan: an appendix that addresses the process of writing and the thinking that must precede and accompany writing.

Keyboard Diagram, Selected PC-Write messages, and Quick Reference: these references are provided to make it easier to use the PC-Write software.

Data Disk: a disk is available to instructors which contains both student files (the document files needed for the Guided Activities and the Applications), and instructor files (the solutions to the Guided Activities and Applications). If you need additional information about this data disk, a demonstration data disk is available which includes files from each of the initial software lab manuals in THE MICROCOMPUTING SERIES. Instructors wishing to request a copy should write to: College Department, West Publishing Company, 50 West Kellogg Boulevard, P.O. Box 64526, St. Paul, MN 55164-1003, or contact their West sales representative.

HOW TO USE THIS BOOK

Unit 1 provides an introduction to word processing concepts, and Units 2 through 5 provide the basis for productive use of PC-Write. These units should be covered first and in the sequence presented. Beyond Unit 5, the units can be covered in the order which best suits current needs.

Here is an overview of each unit:

Unit 1 The Elements of Word Processing: Discusses the elements of a word processor, word processing terminology, and the conventions used in this text.

Unit 2 The PC-Write Operating Environment: Covers keyboard and cursor control, making copies of the the PC-Write disks, and making working and data disks.

Unit 3 Loading and Editing a Document: Loading and saving a document, cursor control, and the Edit Status line.

Unit 4 Creating a Document: Creating a new document, checking spelling, inserting the current date, and setting page breaks, and printing a document.

Unit 5 Saving and Printing a Document: Saving a document with a different file name, printing with double spacing between lines, and printing with keyboard input.

Unit 6 Text and Page Formatting: Using an edit control file, creating headers, footers, and footnotes, and printing page numbers.

Unit 7 Copying and Moving Text: Copying text within and between documents, and moving text.

Unit 8 Finding and Replacing Text: Locating existing text and replacing it with new text, setting the cursor.

Unit 9 Enhancing Text: Causing characters (i.e letters, numbers, and other symbols), words, lines, and blocks of text to stand out through underlining, boldfacing, enlarging, reducing, and enclosing.

Unit 10 Integrated Operations--Windows and File Insertion: Looking at using two different parts of the same or different documents at the same time, inserting database and spreadsheet files into a document.

Unit 11 Integrated Operations--Merging: Combining one document with another document to produce a third document.

A NOTE OF THANKS.....

to Rosalie; Ann Camille; Barbara and Eddie; Daphne, Joe, and Lauren Ann; Catherine and Victor; Mary, and, in memory, John; students, and colleagues who in many ways contributed to the writing of the book;

to Rich Wohl, Rebecca Wee, and Beth Bulger of West Publishing for their timely support and guidance;

to the reviewers, Jeffrey D. Ritter of St. Norbert College, Carol Asplund of the College of Lake County, Cynthia Kachik of Santa Fe Community College, Dolores Pusins of Hillsborough Community College, and Bernard Zalewski of the University of Dayton, for their helpful and supportive comments.

to David Guest, President of Beaman Porter Inc., publishers of **PowerText Formatter**, *Software for Automatic DeskTop Publishing*. His help in using the PowerText Formatter, along with Inset 2 from APG Software for capturing screen images, resulted in high-quality camera-ready copy.

VPM
Deer Park, N.Y.
Fall, 1987

1

FUNDAMENTAL WORD PROCESSING OPERATIONS

This first of three parts discusses the elements of a word processor, the PC-Write operating environment, loading and editing a document, creating a new document, and saving and printing a document.

1

THE ELEMENTS OF WORD PROCESSING

LEARNING OBJECTIVES

Upon completion of this unit you should understand

1. the elements of a word processor.

2. word processing terms.

3. the conventions used in this text.

UNIT OUTLINE

Learning Objectives

Unit Outline

Introduction

The Elements of a Word Processor

    Microcomputer

    Word Processing Program

    You

Word Processing Terms

Textbook Conventions

Review Questions

INTRODUCTION

PC-Write is a computer program which allows you to create, edit, and print documents. PC-Write requires a microcomputer and a microcomputer user to perform its tasks. This unit discusses how the microcomputer, the PC-Write computer program, and the user work together to produce documents.

THE ELEMENTS OF A WORD PROCESSOR

A word processor is an electronic system which allows the creation, editing, and printing of documents. A word processor has three parts: a microcomputer, including a printer; a word processing program that is stored in the computer's memory; and you, the user.

MICROCOMPUTER

A microcomputer is a machine that allows a person to accomplish useful work. That work may be supplying special instructions to the computer to accomplish a given task (called **programming**); storing data in a file (called **database management**); calculating relationships among lists of numbers (called **spreadsheet analysis**); presenting numbers in picture form (called **graphics**); exchanging data with other machines or people (called **communications**); or preparing documents that contain text (called **word processing**).

A microcomputer system consists of a **central processing unit** (CPU), **input devices**, **output devices**, and **storage media** and **devices**. The CPU contains electronic parts that can store programs as well as information, such as, the text of a document.

An example of an input device is a keyboard (similar to that found on a typewriter). The letters on the keys you strike are stored in computer memory. Examples of output devices are the monitor and the printer. The text stored in memory is shown on the monitor's TV-like screen and printed out on paper. An example of a storage medium is a magnetic disk. The text in memory may be transferred to a magnetic disk file and recalled into memory at a later date. The device that does the recording and playing back of disk text files is called a disk drive. Additional information on microcomputetrs can be found in Appendix A.

WORD PROCESSING PROGRAM

A word processing program is a series of instructions that are loaded into the computer's memory. The series of instructions is called a **program**. The program allows the computer to accept your words (text) from the keyboard, place them in memory, output them to the printer, and store the text on a disk for later use.

A word processing program is also a particular kind of software package. A software package usually consists of a program disk and an operating manual. A word processing software package can allow you to do the following:

Create a document file in the computer's memory

Edit (change) the text file

Save or store the text file on a magnetic disk

Print the text file

Recall the text file from the magnetic disk into the computer's memory for document additions, deletions, updating, or further printing.

Word processing programs can also have features which do these things:

Allow dark and underlined print

Divide the screen in half so you can look at two documents (called windows) at the same time

Check spelling

Count the number of words in a document for style and readability analysis

Provide footnotes, indexes, and tables of contents

Combine (merge) material from one document with material from another document.

The word processing software package used with this book is called PC-Write. It has all of the above features and others as well.

PC-Write uses menus. A **menu** is a list of commands that appear on the computer's monitor. You can cause the menus to appear whenever you wish. This feature will help you learn the basics of PC-Write rather quickly. Menus will be discussed further in the units to come.

YOU

You are the key part in a word processing system. The hardware and software can do nothing unless it has you to do the thinking and the keyboarding (typing). It is you, the user, who must establish a writing purpose, prepare an outline, gather facts, and write. A word processing system can then help you turn your words into a document that is uniform in appearance, easily read, and suitable for distribution.

Figure 1-1 shows the relationship among the elements of a word processor.

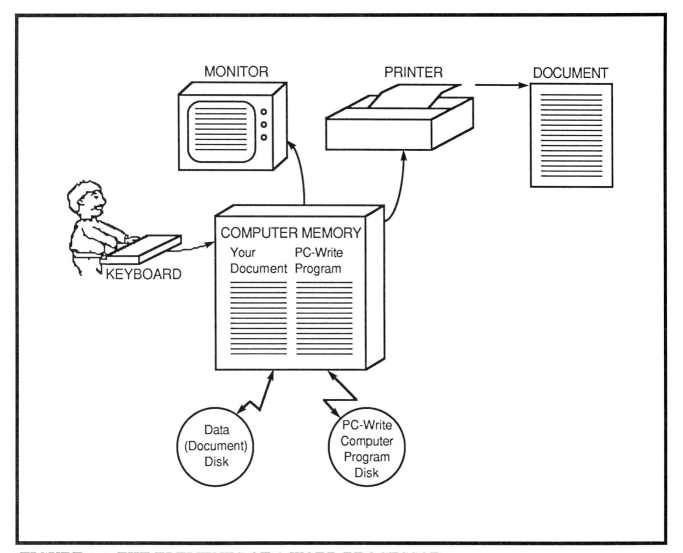

FIGURE 1-1 THE ELEMENTS OF A WORD PROCESSOR

WORD PROCESSING TERMS

Words in sentences and paragraphs are called **text**. Text appears in a **page**. A page, which is also called a **document**, is usually 8 1/2 wide by 11-inches long. A document can be one or more pages in length.

Paragraphs are normally either **right ragged** or **justified**. Right ragged paragraphs are those whose right-side text does not line up. Justified paragraphs are those whose right-side text does line up. Most of the paragraphs in this text are justified.

This paragraph has it's first line **indented**. Indenting is used to show where a new paragraph starts. The degree of indention is called the **paragraph margin**. If a paragraph is not indented, as in the case of the two paragraphs above, double spaces between paragraphs are used to show paragraph separation.

The empty spaces on either side of a page, to the left and right of the text, are referred to as **margins**. Therefore, there is a **left margin** and a **right margin**. In an 8 1/2 by 11-inch page, the left and right margins are usually one-inch wide. Margins can be set as desired.

When a word processor is in the **pushright** mode, text typed on a line pushes any existing text to the right. When a word processor is the the **overwrite** mode, any text that is typed on a line writes over (erases) any existing text on the right.

A word that will not fit completely on the end of a line can be moved automatically to the beginning of the next line. Moving a word in this fashion is called **wordwrap**.

Figure 1-2 shows a typical document produced by a word processor. The document shown represents a business letter prepared in block format. A block format letter aligns all the text on the left margin. Formats for other documents are shown in Appendix C.

TEXTBOOK CONVENTIONS

In order to standardize the manner in which instructions are presented to you, the reader, certain conventions will be followed.

1. An IBM-PC or compatible microcomputer with two floppy disk drives is assumed. If you are using a hard disk system all Disk Operating System (DOS) prompts refer to the C: prompt.

2. In the guided activities, any key you are to press is presented in boldface (dark print) and enclosed in brackets: **<Return>**, **<Esc>**, **<Right Arrow>**, and **<Del>**.

3. In the guided activities, anything you are to type or to select from a menu is presented in **boldface**.

4. Function keys F1 through F10 (located on the left side of the keyboard) will not be enclosed in brackets. They will be presented as a capital letter followed by a number: F7.

5. To perform certain functions, combinations of keys must be pressed. Sometimes the keys are pressed one after another. Sometimes one or two keys is held down while another is depressed. In the first case the keys will be shown separately as in <Return> <Pg Up>. In the second case the keys will be connected with a hyphen: <Shift>-<PrtSc>.

6. Instead of saying (for example) "and press the <Pg Up> key" we will say "press <Pg Up>, or "and press <Pg Up>."

7. The phrase "move to" or "point to" or "highlight" means to move the cursor to the location specified.

8. "Select" means point to a menu item and press <Return> or press the function key associated with the menu item.

9. The phrase "turn on the computer system" means turn on all the electrical power switches associated with the computer system hardware.

```
                    SOFTSIDE COMPUTERS
                      One Robin Lane
                 Shelter Island, New York 11964
                      1-800-999-9999




    January 15, 1990



    General Manager
    Building Products Inc.
    123 Sun Drive
    Kerrigan, Florida

    Dear Sir or Madam

    Our new Model 99 StarWhisper computer goes on sale next
    week.  Priced at two thousand dollars, it features
    voice-activated operation and is designed to fit on the
    ring finger.

    Model 99 is energized by human breath.  The breath that
    accompanies your whispered instructions is enough to power
    the unit.  Data is stored on the skin surface of the ring
    finger.  You will need a skin-to-disk conversion device
    ($100.) to permanently store your data.

    Please call 1-800-999-9999 to place your order or to
    arrange for  a demonstration.

    Sincerely


    Ms Ima Kidder
    Sales Manager
```

FIGURE 1-2 A LETTER IN OPEN BLOCK FORMAT STYLE

REVIEW QUESTIONS

1. Describe a word processor.

_____

_____

2. Identify the elements of a word processor.

_____

_____

3. What is PC-Write?

_____

_____

4. Describe eight tasks associated with a word processing program.

_____

_____

_____

_____

_____

_____

_____

_____

5. What is a menu?

_____

_____

6. Here are two lists. Draw a line between an item in the first list and a matching item in the second list.

indent and/or double space	New text pushes exisitng text to the right
justified	new text erases exisitng text on the right
margin	text at right margin is not aligned
document	the space between paper edges and the text
paragraph margin	text on right margin is aligned
pushright	words in a document
right ragged	word is moved to the beginning of next line
overwrite	used to show a new paragraph
text	the degree of paragraph indention
wordwrap	page(s) of text

UNIT

2 THE PC-WRITE OPERATING ENVIRONMENT

LEARNING OBJECTIVES

Upon completion of this unit you should understand

1. the general features of PC-Write.

2. the functions of the PC-Write keyboard.

3. the three classes of keyboard keys.

4. the PC-Write menus.

5. how to install PC-Write on your computer.

14 Understanding and Using PC-Write

UNIT OUTLINE

Learning Objectives

Unit Outline

The PC-Write Word Processing Program

    Introduction

    The Working Disk and the Data Disk

    Operational Summary

The PC-Write Keyboard

    Keyboard Functions

    The Cursor and the Keyboard

    Keyboard Keys

        Text Keys

        Cursor Control Keys

        Command Keys

The PC-Write Menus

Copying the PC-Write Program and Utility Disks

    Installation Activity 1 Copying the PC-Write Disks

Installing PC-Write on a Floppy Disk System

    Installation Activity 2 Making a Working Disk

    Installation Activity 3 Making a Data Disk

Installing PC-Write on a Hard Disk System

    Installation Activity 4 Making a Working/Data Directory

Configuring PC-Write for More Than One Printer

    Floppy Disk System

    Hard Disk System

Review Questions

THE PC-Write WORD PROCESSING PROGRAM

INTRODUCTION

PC-Write version 2.71 comes on two 5 1/4-inch, double-sided, double-density, floppy disks. One disk is the System disk and the other is the Utility disk. These two disks are used to create a working disk. PC-Write includes an edit program which allows you to create documents and a print program which allows you to print documents. Version 2.71 includes these features: a) a 50,000 word spelling checker, b) the ability to import text from other programs, c) a date/time function, and d) advanced text formatting options.

THE WORKING DISK AND THE DATA DISK

The working disk, which you create, contains the most frequently used PC-Write programs. The spelling checker and help screens can also be installed on the working disk. The working disk is used in day-to-day operations. In a floppy disk system, the working disk is placed in drive A. A formatted data disk, which will store your document files, is placed in drive B.

Instructions for creating working and data disks are given later in this unit.

OPERATIONAL SUMMARY

Here is an operational summary of PC-Write, Version 2.71.

Computer Memory Size	Maximum size of PC-Write Document File	Availability of Spelling Checker
64K	(cannot use PC-Write)	
128K	5K	No
256K	60K	No
320K	60K	Yes

THE PC-Write KEYBOARD

KEYBOARD FUNCTIONS

The keyboard is your communications link to the personal computer. Through it you enter text into a document and command the PC-Write program. Each letter or number keystroke you make causes the computer to store the letter or number (called a **character**) in its memory. Figure 2-1 is an illustration of the keyboard.

Other keystrokes cause PC-Write to perform specific functions, such as copying a document from computer memory to disk (called **saving**) or copying a document from computer memory to paper (called **printing**).

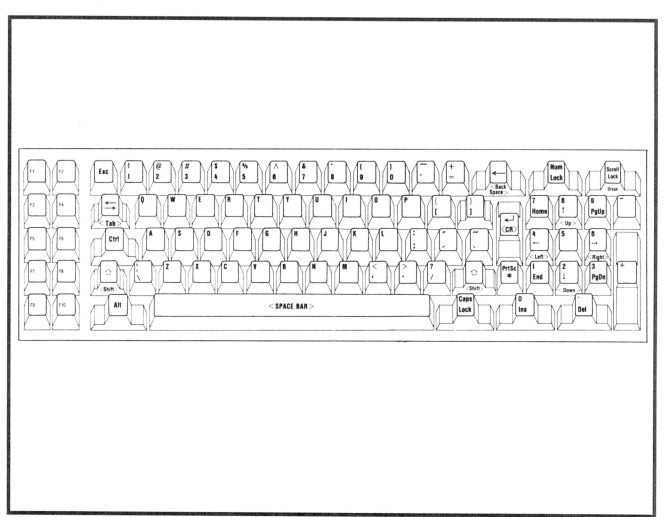

FIGURE 2-1 KEYBOARD ILLUSTRATION

THE CURSOR AND THE KEYBOARD

When PC-Write is operating, the screen shows a small bright flashing rectangle. The bright rectangle is called a cursor. "Cursor" comes from the Latin word meaning "to move."

The cursor shows where the next character you type (letter, number or other symbol) will appear on the screen. When you press a key, the cursor moves to the right. The letter or number you type appears in the cursor's former position. As you enter characters from the keyboard, they appear on the screen and the cursor keeps moving to the right. You can always tell where the next character will appear by looking at the cursor position.

KEYBOARD KEYS

Not every keyboard key will move the cursor. That is because there are three types of keys: **text** keys, **cursor control** keys, and PC- Write **command** keys.

Although there are exceptions, the **text** keys are generally the letter and number keys in the middle and across the top of the keyboard. You use these keys to enter text in your document.

The **cursor control** keys are primarily on the right side of the keyboard. They are the up/down and right/left arrow keys, and the PgUp and PgDn keys. You use these keys to move the cursor anywhere on the screen.

The **command** keys are primarily the grey keys on the left and right sides of the keyboard. For example, you use these keys to command PC-Write to save a document, print a document, switch files, reformat your text, and locate a specific word.

Text Keys You enter text, including punctuation marks and special symbols, by using the keys shown in Table 2-1.

TABLE 2-1 Keys for Entering Text

Text Type	Key
Letters and Numbers	**Upper case letters A through Z** **Lower case letters a through z** **Numbers 0 through 9**
Punctuation Marks	**! (exclamation point)** **' (apostrophe)** **((left parenthesis)** **~ (tilde)** **) (right parenthesis)** **' (accent mark)** **_ (underscore)** **, (comma)** **- (hyphen)** **. (period)** **: (colon)** **? (question mark)** **; (semi-colon)** **space bar (blank)** **" (double quotation mark)**

TABLE 2-1 Keys for Entering Text (Continued)

Text Type	Key
Special Symbols	@ (at)
	= (equal)
	# (pound or number)
	{ (left curly bracket)
	$ (dollar)
	[(left square bracket)
	% (percent)
	} (right curly bracket)
	^ (caret)
	] (right square bracket)
	& (and)
	\ (back slash)
	* (asterisk)
	/ (forward slash)
	+ (plus)
	< (less-than symbol, also used as bracket)
	> (greater-than symbol, also used as bracket)

To enter a capital letter, hold down either shift key and press the desired letter. The shift keys have an upward-pointing fat arrow on them. They are above and to the left and right of the space bar. The space bar is the long key at the bottom of the keyboard. To enter all capital letters, first press the **Caps Lock** key to the right of the space bar. Everything typed will then be in capital letters. To return to lowercase, press the **Caps Lock** key again.

Numbers can be entered by using keys 0 through 9 across the top of the keyboard. They can also be entered by using the numeric keypad on the right side of the keyboard. To use the keypad for numbers, first press the **Num Lock** key on the upper right side of the keyboard. This locks the keypad into supplying numbers only. To unlock the keypad, press the **Num Lock** key again. As a general rule, you should use the number keys on the top row of the keyboard. This will avoid having to press the Num Lock key to switch between the number keys and the cursor control keys.

Some punctuation marks and special symbols appear on the top part of a key. To enter one of these, hold down a shift key and press the punctuation mark or special symbol you want.

Cursor Control Keys You can position the cursor on the screen as shown in Table 2-2.

TABLE 2-2 Positioning the Cursor

Key	Keyboard Location	Function
<Tab>	Left side	Moves cursor to right a predetermined number of spaces. Moves cursor to left if shift key held down and Tab key pressed.
<Backspace>	Right side	Moves cursor to left. Erases letters in its path.
<Enter>	Right side	Moves cursor from right side of screen to to left side of screen on next line. Also enters text in computer's memory.
<Ins> (Insert)	Right side	Inserts a space.
<Del> (Delete)	Right side	When pressed, will delete the letter the cursor is on. Will keep deleting if held down.
<End>	Keypad	Moves cursor to right side of current line.
<Down Arrow>	Keypad	Moves cursor down one line.
<PgDn>	Keypad	Shows next line at bottom of screen.
<Left Arrow>	Keypad	Moves cursor one position to left.
<Right Arrow>	Keypad	Moves cursor one position to right.
<Home>	Keypad	Moves cursor to left side of current line.
<Up Arrow>	Keypad	Moves cursor up one line.
<PgUp>	Keypad	Shows previous line at top of screen.

There are other ways to control the cursor location. They are discussed in Unit 3 and other units throughout the text.

Command Keys The command keys allow you to instruct PC-Write to perform editing functions. They are used by themselves or in combination with other function keys. These are the command keys:

  The ten function keys marked F1 through F10.
  The <Alt>, <Shift>, <Ctrl>, and <Esc> keys.

Table 2-3 contains examples of using these keys to command PC-Write.

TABLE 2-3 Examples of Command Keys

Pressing These Keys:	Results in this:
<Ctrl> and F3	Ability to insert a file
<Ctrl> and F8	Making text move flush right
<Shift> and F8	Centering text on a line

There are actually hundreds of commands that you can give PC-Write. Each one performs a different task. If this sounds overwhelming, it is--especially when you are first learning to use PC-Write.

However, you will easily learn to command PC-Write for these reasons:

  Only a few commands are needed to perform the essential tasks of entering text, editing text, and printing documents.

  PC-Write provides useful help screens. You call up the help screens by pressing Function key F1 when in the **edit mode** (i.e. when entering text), or by pressing function key F1 when the System/Help menu is on the screen. See Figure 2-2.

  PC-Write has menus which you can display on the screen. You can use the menus to execute commands, or you can use command keys. The commands will become second nature the more you use PC-Write.

  You have this book to help you. You will find that the text will first discuss the meaning of a function, then provide the general procedure for using the function, and finally provide a guided activity in the use of the function.

THE PC-Write MENUS

A **menu** is a list containing choices. In PC-Write, the choices represent various word processing commands. Figure 2-2 shows the PC- Write System/Help menu. A menu choice can be made by pressing the associated function key. A menu choice can also be made by moving the cursor to the menu item (by using <Right Arrow> or <Left Arrow>) and pressing <Enter>. Moving the cursor in this manner is called **pointing** or **highlighting**.

When a menu item (also called a **command**) is highlighted, the message line below the menu describes the command's function. For example, Figure 2-2 has the command **F5-Name** highlighted. The message line says, "Enter new filename to use when saving text to disk." As different commands are highlighted, the message changes. Only when <Enter> or the associated function key is pressed is the command executed.

```
Esc F1:Help   F2.Exit   F3.Save  F4.Command  F5:Name F6:File  F7:Print  F8:Dir   F9:Unsave

Enter new filename to use when saving text to disk
```

FIGURE 2-2 THE PC-Write SYSTEM/HELP MENU

Commands can also be implemented by pressing the appropriate command keys. It is not necessary for the associated menu to be on the screen. Figure 2-3 shows the PC-Write Alt main menu. This menu is brought to the screen by pressing <Esc> and then <Alt> when in the edit mode. Commands in this menu can be executed by pressing a function key or by pointing. However, the Alt main menu does not have to be on the screen to execute one of its commands.

Notice the small "a" next to each function key. The small a represents the <Alt> key. If you hold down <Alt> and press a corresponding function key, the associated command will be executed-- even if the Alt main menu is not on the screen.

```
aF1:Name/File  aF3:Key-record  aF5:Conversion  a7:Pagebreaks  aF9:To-Location
aF2:Spelling   aF4:Misc-stuff              aF8:Upper-case  aF10.Replace-all
```

FIGURE 2-3 THE PC-Write ALT MAIN MENU

Should you work through menus or command keys? It depends upon how familiar you are with PC-Write. Command keys are quicker, if you know the key sequence. Otherwise you can search the menus for the function you want. Since there are hundreds of functions in PC-Write, you will probably use a combination approach. Additional PC-Write menus are shown in Appendix D.

The remainder of this unit is devoted to getting ready to use PC-Write. If you have a floppy disk system, perform installation activities 1,2, and 3. If you have a hard disk system, perform installation activities 1 and 4. If you will be using more than one printer with PC-Write, see the section "Configuring PC-Write For More Than One Printer" at the end of this unit.

COPYING THE PC-Write PROGRAM AND UTILITY DISKS

The PC-Write copyright requires that each user be supplied with a complete copy of the PC-Write disks. This section contains the procedure for making a copy of the PC-Write Program disk and the PC- Write Utility disk.

INSTALLATION ACTIVITY 1   COPYING THE PC-Write DISKS

This procedure requires a DOS disk and two blank, double-sided, double-density, 5 1/4-inch floppy disks. You will also need to obtain the PC-Write Program and Utility disks from your instructor or from the laboratory technical assistant.

1. Insert a DOS disk in drive A, turn on the computer system, and enter the date and time.

2. Verify that the A> prompt is on the screen.

3. Type **DISKCOPY A: B:** and press **<Enter>**.

4. Insert the PC-Write Program disk in drive A.

5. Insert a new disk in drive B and press any key. After a minute or so the contents of the Program disk will be copied to the disk in drive B.

6. Label the disk in drive B "PC-Write Program disk."

7. Notice that DOS is asking if you want to make another copy.

8. Type **N** for No.

9. Insert a DOS disk in drive A and type **DISKCOPY A: B:** and press **<Enter>**.

10. Insert the PC-Write Utility disk in drive A.

11. Insert a new disk in drive B and press any key. The contents of the Utility disk are copied to the disk in drive B. Answer N for No when asked if you want to make another copy.

12. Label the disk in drive B "PC-Write Utility disk."

13. Return the laboratory copy of the PC-Write Program and Utility disks to your instructor or to the laboratory technical assistant.

You have now completed copying the PC-Write Program and Utility disks. You are now ready to install PC-Write on a floppy disk or hard disk system.

INSTALLING PC-Write ON A FLOPPY DISK SYSTEM

The PC-Write word processor actually consists of two major programs. One program, ED.EXE, allows you to create and edit documents. The other, PR.EXE, allows you to print documents. Both of these program files are on the Program disk. The Program disk also contains a file which allows you to control document margins (ED.DEF) and a file which provides on-screen help (ED.HLP). These four files will be transferred to a disk which will be called the working disk.

The Utility disk contains a file which allows you to tell PC-Write which printer you are using and a file which contains the 50,000 word spelling checker. These files will also be transferred to your working disk. Once created, the working disk is used in day-to-day operations.

INSTALLATION ACTIVITY 2   MAKING A WORKING DISK

This procedure requires a DOS disk, your copy of the PC-Write Program disk, and your copy of the PC-Write Utility disk. You will also need one blank, double-sided, 5 1/4-inch, floppy disk. The blank disk will serve as your working disk.

In this procedure you will format the working disk with the FORMAT command. You will then transfer the necessary files from the Program and Utility disks to the working disk. During the procedure you will be asked to replace the Program disk with the Utility disk and to specify the printer you are using. Follow the instructions on the screen.

1. Insert a DOS disk (version 2.x or 3.x) in drive A, turn on the computer system, and enter the date and time. Place a new disk in drive B.

2. Verify that the A> prompt is on the screen.

3. Type **FORMAT B:** and press **<Enter>**. After a minute or so, the disk in drive B is formatted. When asked if you want to format another disk, answer N for No.

4. Remove the DOS disk from drive A and insert the PC-Write Program disk in drive A.

5. Type **WORKDISK B:** and press <Enter>.

   a) The Workdisk program copies the ED.EXE and PR.EXE files to the working disk in drive B.

   b) When you are asked if you want the Help screens, answer Y for Yes. The ED.DEF and ED.HLP files are then copied to the working disk.

c) You are asked a question about your computer set-up. After you answer, you are asked if you have a copy of the PC-Write utility disk. Answer Y for Yes. You are then asked to place the utility disk in drive A.

d) Answer the questions regarding your printer set-up.

e) You are asked another question about your computer set-up and then asked whether you want the spelling checker word list. If your computer has *at least 320K* of user memory, answer Y for Yes. Otherwise, answer N for No.

6. Your PC-Write Working disk is now ready for use. Remove it from drive B and label it "PC-Write Working Disk, Version 2.71."

INSTALLATION ACTIVITY 3   MAKING A DATA DISK

This procedure requires a DOS disk and one blank, double-sided, double-density, 5 1/4-inch floppy disk. You will also need to obtain the *Understanding and Using PC-Write* sample files data disk from your instructor or from the laboratory technical assistant.

In this procedure you will format the blank disk with the FORMAT/S command. This will allow you to boot the computer with the data disk. You will not need a separate DOS disk to boot the computer. The /S parameter is added to the data disk because the data disk, and not the working disk, has the additional space required by the /S parameter. (Although not necessary at this time, you may want to refer to Figure C-2 in Appendix C for additional information on formatting a floppy disk with the /S parameter.)

The data disk will hold the sample files necessary to complete this text's guided activities. The sample files all have a file extension of either .DOC or .WK1. The data disk will also hold the files you create.

1. Insert a DOS disk in drive A, turn on the computer system, and enter the date and time.

2. Verify that the A> prompt is on the screen.

3. Type **FORMAT B:/S** and press **<Enter>**.

4. Place a new disk in drive B and press any key. After a minute or so, the disk in drive B will be formatted. When asked if you want to format another disk, answer N for No.

5. Remove the DOS disk from drive A and and insert the *Understanding and Using PC-Write* data disk in drive A.

6. Type **COPY *.DOC B:** and press <Enter>. The sample files for the guided activities are now copied to the data disk in drive B.

7. Type **COPY *.WK1 B:** and press **<Enter>**. The sample spreadsheet file for the guided activities is now copied to the data disk in drive B.

8. Remove the disk in drive B and label it "PC-Write Data Disk." Return the laboratory copy of the data disk to your instructor or to the laboratory technical assistant.

You now have a document data disk. With it and your working disk, you are prepared to perform the guided activities which begin in Unit 3.

INSTALLING PC-Write ON A HARD DISK SYSTEM

INSTALLATION ACTIVITY 4   MAKING A WORKING/DATA DIRECTORY

This procedure requires a formatted hard disk, your copy of the PC-Write Program disk, and your copy of the PC-Write Utility disk. You will also need to obtain the *Understanding and Using PC-Write* data disk from your instructor or from the laboratory technical assistant.

In this procedure you will make a PC-Write directory. You will then place the PC-Write working files, and the *Understanding and Using PC-Write* data files in the directory.

1. Turn on the computer system.

2. Enter the date and time and verify that the C> prompt is on the screen.

3. Type **MKDIR PCWRITE** and press <Enter>. This creates a directory called PCWRITE. This directory will hold the PC-Write working files and data files.

4. Type **A:** and press **<Enter>**. Verify that the A> prompt is on the screen.

5. Insert the PC-Write Program disk in drive A.

6. Type **WORKDISK C:\PCWRITE** and press **<Enter>**.

   a) The Workdisk program copies the ED.EXE and PR.EXE files to the PCWRITE directory.

   b) When you are asked if you want the Help screens, answer Y for Yes. The ED.DEF and ED.HLP files are then copied to the PCWRITE directory.

   c) You are asked a question about your computer set-up. After you answer, you are asked if you have a copy of the PC-Write utility disk. Answer Y for Yes. You are then asked to place the utility disk in drive A.

   d) Answer the questions regarding your printer set-up.

e) You are asked another question about your computer set-up and then asked whether you want the spelling checker word list. If your computer has *at least 320K* of user memory, answer Y for Yes. Otherwise, answer N or No.

7. Insert the *Understanding and Using PC-Write* data disk in drive A.

8. Type: **COPY *.DOC C:\PCWRITE** and press **<Enter>**. The sample data files for the guided activities are now copied to the directory.

9. Type **COPY *.WK1 C:\PCWRITE** and press **<Enter>**. The sample spreadwheet file for the guided activities is now copied to the hard disk. Return the laboratory copy of the data disk to your instructor or to the laboratory technical assistant.

You now have a working/data directory called PC-Write and are prepared to perform the guided activities which begin in Unit 3.

CONFIGURING PC-Write FOR MORE THAN ONE PRINTER

Perform the procedure described in this section only if you expect to use PC-Write with more than one type of printer.

When you prepared your working disk or directory, a print control file (PR.DEF) was placed on the disk or directory. The PR.DEF contains the printer control settings for the printer you specified. If you will be using more than one printer model, you must create a separate printer control file for each different printer.

None of the printer control file names you create can use the name PR.DEF. When preparing to print, the PC-Write print program automatically looks for the file name PR.DEF. If a PR.DEF file is found, the print program will ignore any other printer control file name. Therefore, you must allow PC-Write to look for unique printer control file names, each representing a different printer model.

FLOPPY DISK SYSTEM

To configure your working disk to work with more than one printer, proceed as follows:

1. Bring the DOS A> prompt to the screen.

2. Place your PC-Write utility disk in drive A and your PC-Write working disk in drive B.

3. Type **DEL B:PR.DEF** and press **<Enter>** to delete the PR.DEF printer control file from your working disk.

4. Type **MENUPRT B:filename** and press **<Enter>**. For "filename" use the name of your printer. The "filename" cannot exceed eight characters. Do not use the file name PR.DEF.

   For example, if one of your printers is an IBM Graphics printer, you could type MENUPRT B:IBMGRAPH and press <Enter>. Then select the IBM Graphics printer from among the choices that appear on the screen

5. Repeat Step 4 for each different printer. Each "filename" must be different. Do not use PR.DEF as a file name.

   When you use the print program, you will be asked to enter a printer control file name since the print program will not be able to find the file PR.DEF. At that point, enter one of the printer control file names you created.

HARD DISK SYSTEM

1. Bring the DOS C> prompt to the screen.

2. Type **CD PCWRITE** and press **<Enter>** to change to the PC-Write directory.

3. Type **DEL C:PR.DEF** and press **<Enter>** to delete the PR.DEF printer control file from the directory.

4. Type **A:** and press **<Enter>** to bring the A> prompt to the screen.

5. Insert your copy of the PC-Write utility disk in drive A.

6. Do steps 4 and 5 in the floppy disk procedure immediately above except substitute C: for B:.

REVIEW QUESTIONS

1. Identify the three types of PC-Write keys.

   _____

   _____

   _____

2. Where, on the keyboard, are the cursor control keys located?

   _____

3. Where, on the keyboard, are the command keys located?

_____

4. How many keys must be pressed to bring up the Alt main menu?

_____

5. Enter the choices that appear on the PC-Write System/Help menu.

_____

_____

_____

_____

_____

_____

_____

_____

_____

6. Use the DOS DIR command and enter the file names (include extensions) that appear on your PC-Write working disk.

_____

_____

_____

_____

_____

_____

_____

_____

_____

7. Use the DOS DIR command and enter the file names (include extensions) that appear on your data disk.

_____

_____

_____

_____

_____

_____

_____

_____

_____

_____

3

LOADING AND EDITING A DOCUMENT

LEARNING OBJECTIVES

Upon completion of this unit you should understand how to

1. load a document file from disk into computer memory.

2. set temporary margins with the ruler line.

3. control the cursor.

4. use the edit status line.

5. add and delete text.

6. reformat a paragraph.

7. save a document.

UNIT OUTLINE

INTRODUCTION

This unit and those that follow have a common pattern. An explanation of a PC-Write function is presented first. This is followed by a description of the general procedure for implementing that function using PC-Write. The general procedures are followed by guided activities in which you actually use the functions being discussed.

GETTING PC-WRITE READY

Before PC-Write can be used, the A> prompt must be on the screen, a PC-Write working disk must be in drive A, and a data disk should be in drive B. If you have not prepared working and data disks, refer to Installation Activities 2 and 3 in Unit 2.

Follow the steps in Figure 3-1 to get PC-Write ready to use.

- Bring the DOS A> prompt to the screen.

- Insert a PC-Write working disk in drive A.

- Insert a document data disk in drive B.

FIGURE 3-1 GETTING PC-Write READY TO USE

From this point on, the phrase "Get PC-Write Ready," means you should perform the three steps shown in Figure 3-1.

GENERAL PROCEDURES

This section contains general procedures for performing various PC- Write functions. The procedures fall into these general categories:

    Loading a document
    Controlling the Cursor
    Using the Edit Status Line
    Editing Text

Whenever a file name is called for in the following examples, the example file name "Sample.Fil" will be used.

LOADING A DOCUMENT

To Load a File By Typing Its Name at the DOS Prompt

- Get PC-Write ready.
- Type ED B:Sample.Fil and press <Enter>.
- Press <Esc>.

Here is what happens on the screen:

The command **ED** loads the PC-Write edit program into the computer's memory. The characters **B:** tell PC-Write to look at the B drive. **Sample.Fil** is the name of a document on the disk in drive B that is to be loaded into memory.

The message shown in Figure 3-2 appears at the top of the screen.

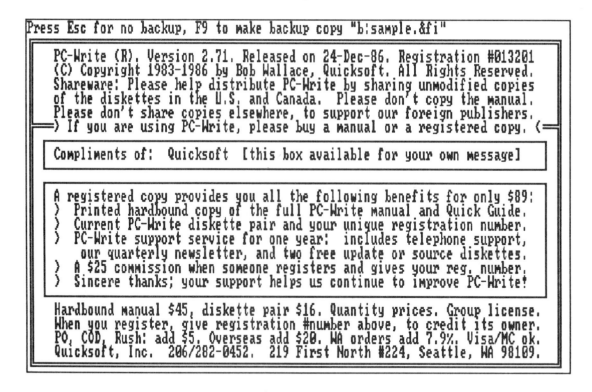

```
Press Esc for no backup, F9 to make backup copy "b:sample.&fi"

 PC-Write (R), Version 2.71, Released on 24-Dec-86, Registration #013201
 (C) Copyright 1983-1986 by Bob Wallace, Quicksoft. All Rights Reserved.
 Shareware: Please help distribute PC-Write by sharing unmodified copies
 of the diskettes in the U.S. and Canada.  Please don't copy the manual.
 Please don't share copies elsewhere, to support our foreign publishers.
=) If you are using PC-Write, please buy a manual or a registered copy. (=

 Compliments of:  Quicksoft [this box available for your own message]

 A registered copy provides you all the following benefits for only $89:
 )  Printed hardbound copy of the full PC-Write manual and Quick Guide.
 )  Current PC-Write diskette pair and your unique registration number.
 )  PC-Write support service for one year:  includes telephone support,
     our quarterly newsletter, and two free update or source diskettes.
 )  A $25 commission when someone registers and gives your reg. number.
 )  Sincere thanks; your support helps us continue to improve PC-Write!

 Hardbound manual $45, diskette pair $16. Quantity prices. Group license.
 When you register, give registration #number above, to credit its owner.
 PO, COD, Rush: add $5. Overseas add $20. WA orders add 7.9%. Visa/MC ok.
 Quicksoft, Inc.  206/282-0452.  219 First North #224, Seattle, WA 98109.
```

FIGURE 3-2 THE PC-Write "HELLO" SCREEN WHEN AN <u>EXISTING</u> FILE (SAMPLE.FIL) IS LOADED BY TYPING ED B:SAMPLE.FIL AT THE DOS PROMPT

The **&** symbol in the file name extension denotes a backup file. You now have the choice either to make a backup copy of the file by pressing function key F9 or to directly enter the file by pressing the <Esc> key. In our guided activities, we will directly enter the file by pressing the <Esc> key.

Pressing the <Esc> key causes the document to appear on the screen. The top line or edit status line shown in Figure 3-3 appears at the top of the screen.

Esc:Menu@Push Wrap+Sp- X% Free. Y% Thru. Read "b:sample.fil"

[the contents of the document fill the rest of the screen]

FIGURE 3-3 THE EDIT STATUS LINE

You can now edit your document. An explanation of the edit status line appears below under "Using the Edit Status Line."

To Load a File Without Typing Its Name at the DOS Prompt

- Get PC-Write ready.
- Type ED and press <Enter>.
- Press F8 to select "F8:Dir."
- Type B: and press <Enter> to display the file name directory for the disk in the B drive.
- Use the cursor arrow keys to highlight the name of the file you want to load.
- Press <Enter> to load the selected file.
- Press <Esc> to display the document on the screen.

Here is what happens on the screen.

The command **ED** loads the PC-Write edit program into the computer's memory. The message shown in Figure 3-4 appears at the top of the screen.

File to load or create (Esc:cancel F8:dir): "work.doc"

[The rest of the screen is the same as Figure 3-2.]

FIGURE 3-4 THE PC-Write "HELLO" SCREEN WHEN *ED* IS TYPED AT THE DOS PROMPT

Pressing **F8**, typing **B:**, and pressing **<Enter>** causes PC-Write to display the file name directory of the data disk in drive B. See Figure 3-5.

BF.DOC	4	7-24-87	6:10a
POPUL.DOC	1188	7-27-87	7:35a
FILLBAL.DOC	582	7-11-87	4:47a
DECLARA.DOC	5934	11-01-86	7:25p
NOTRIGHT.DOC	4740	7-27-87	10:56a
EDITME.DOC	1960	7-09-87	1:52a
GUIDED\	0	7-02-87	12:36p

FIGURE 3-5 A SAMPLE PC-Write DIRECTORY LISTING

Highlighting a file name with the cursor arrow keys, and then pressing **<Enter>**, loads the selected file into memory. At this point, the procedure is the same as if the file had been loaded directly from the DOS prompt. Pressing <Esc> displays the document on the screen, as shown in Figure 3-3.

To Load a File When Another File is Already Loaded

■ With a document already loaded, and with the edit status line on the screen (see Figure 3-3), press F1 to bring up the System/Help menu.
■ Press F6 to select "File."
■ Press F8 to select "Dir."
■ Type B: and press <Enter> to display the file name directory for the disk in the B drive.
■ Use the cursor arrow keys to highlight the name of the file you want to load.
■ Press <Enter> to load the selected file. The original file is saved to the disk.
■ Press <Esc> to display the loaded document on the screen.

To Set Temporary Left and Right Margins With The Ruler Line

The ruler line controls the margins in your document. PC-Write automatically sets the left and right margins at columns 1 and 78, but you can change these settings.

You can bring the ruler line to the screen by pressing F2 when in the edit mode. You can then set the margins by typing directly on the ruler line. A capital L is typed where you want the left margin to be. A capital R is typed where you want the right margin to be. Here is the sequence.

■ Verify that a document is on the screen and that the Edit Status line (Figure 3-3) is at the top of the screen.
■ Press F2.
■ Move the cursor (using the left and right arrow keys) to the column where you want the left margin and type a capital L.
■ Move the cursor to the column where you want the right margin and type a capital R.
■ Press F2.
■ Start or continue typing.

■ Start or continue typing.

Here is what happens on the screen:

Pressing F2 in the edit mode brings the default ruler line to the screen.

Typing capitals L and R in new columns turns the original capitals L and R in columns 1 and 78 to lower case. This action disables them as margin-setters.

Pressing F2 removes the default ruler line from the screen. The new margins are set. The text you now type will fall between the new settings. When you quit PC-Write, or use the print program, the temporary ruler line settings are lost. Therefore, temporary ruler lines must be reset whenever you re-enter PC-Write or use the print program. Additional information on ruler lines, including setting permanent ruler lines, is contained in Unit 4, Creating a Document.

SAVING A DOCUMENT

To Save and Continue Editing

■ Press F1 to bring up the System/Help menu.
■ Press F3 to select "Save."

To Save and Quit PC-Write

■ Press F1 to bring up the System/Help menu.
■ Press F2 to select "Exit."

GUIDED ACTIVITY 1 LOADING A DOCUMENT, AND SETTING TEMPORARY MARGINS

In this guided activity we will practice three different ways to load a document file. We will also practice setting temporary left and right margins.

PART 1 LOADING A DOCUMENT BY TYPING ITS NAME AT THE DOS PROMPT

1. Get PC-Write ready (Ref. Figure 3-1).

2. Type **ED B:BF.DOC** and press **<Enter>**.

3. Press **<Esc>** to bring the document to the screen.

4. Press **F2** to bring the ruler line to the screen. Type a capital **L** at column 10, and type a capital **R** at column 72. Your ruler line should look like the one shown in Figure 3-6.

5. Press **F2** to remove the ruler line from the screen. Margins have now been set temporarily at columns 10 and 72. If you were to add text to this file (we will not add any text now), the text would fall between columns 10 and 72.

6. Press F1, then F2 to quit PC-Write.

PART 2 LOADING A FILE WITHOUT TYPING ITS NAME AT THE DOS PROMPT

1. Get PC-Write ready (Ref. Figure 3-1).

2. Type **ED** and press **<Enter>** to load the PC-Write edit program into the computer's memory.

3. Press **F8** to select "Dir".

4. Type **B:** and press **<Enter>** to display the directory of file names on the disk in drive B.

5. Press **<Down Arrow>** and highlight the file name **POPUL.DOC**.

6. Press **<Enter>** to load the file.

7. Press **<Esc>** to display the document on the screen.

8. Press **F2** to bring the ruler line to the screen. Type a capital **L** at column 10, and type a capital **R** at column 72.

9. Press **F2** to remove the ruler line from the screen. Margins have now been set temporarily at columns 10 and 72. If we were to add text to this file (we will not add any text now), the text would fall between columns 10 and 72.

10. Go to step 1, Part 3.

PART 3 LOADING A FILE WHEN ANOTHER FILE IS ALREADY LOADED

1. Press **F1** to bring up the System/help menu.

2. Press **F6** to select "**File**" from the menu.

3. Press **F8** to select "**Dir.**"

4. Type **B:** and press **<Enter>** to display the directory of file names on the disk in drive B.

5. Press **<Down Arrow>** and highlight the file name **BF.DOC**.

6. Press **<Enter>** to load the file.

7. Press **<Esc>** to display the file on the screen.

8. Press **F2** to bring the ruler line to the screen. Since we did not first quit PC-Write, notice that the margins have remained set at 10 and 72.

9. Press **F2** to remove the ruler line from the screen.

10. Press F1, then F2 to quit PC-Write.

CHECKPOINT What is the command to load an existing document directly from the DOS prompt?

```
I--------L---+-T--2----T----3--T-+----4T---+---T5----+-T--6----T----7-R--+----I
```

FIGURE 3-6 THE RULER LINE WITH MARGINS SET AT COLUMNS 10 AND 72

CONTROLLING THE CURSOR

SUMMARY OF CURSOR MOVEMENTS

Key	Cursor moves
\<Right Arrow\>	one character to right
\<Left Arrow\>	one character to left
\<Ctrl\> and \<Right Arrow\>	one word to right
\<Ctrl\> and \<Left Arrow\>	one word to left
\<End\>	to end of line
\<Home\>	to beginning of line
\<Down Arrow\>	down one line
\<Up Arrow\>	up one line
\<PgUp\>	shows previous line at top of screen
\<PgDn\>	shows next line at bottom of screen
\<Shift\> and \<Ctrl\> then \<Right Arrow\>	to period of next <u>sentence</u>
\<Shift\> and \<Ctrl\> then \<Left Arrow\>	to period of previous <u>sentence</u>
\<Ctrl\> and \<PgDn\>	to next <u>paragraph</u>
\<Ctrl\> and \<PgUp\>	to previous <u>paragraph</u>
\<Shift\> and \<PgDn\>	down 24 lines (one screen)
\<Shift\> and \<PgUp\>	up 24 lines (one screen)
✒ **\<Alt\> and \<White + \>**	to top of <u>document</u>
✒ **\<Alt\> and \<White -\>**	to end of <u>document</u>

GUIDED ACTIVITY 2   CONTROLLING THE CURSOR

We will bring a sample document to the screen and explore it with the cursor.

1. Get PC-Write ready (Ref. Figure 3-1).

2. Type **ED B:BF.DOC** and press **\<Enter\>**.

3. Press **\<Esc\>**. An excerpt from <u>The Autobiography of Benjamin Franklin</u> is on the screen. Notice that the cursor is in the upper left-hand corner of the screen in column 1.

4. Press **F2** to bring the ruler line to the screen. Type **L** at column 10, type **R** at column 72, and press **F2**.

5. Press **\<Home\>** to bring the cursor to the "E" in "Excerpt."

We will practice moving the cursor <u>one character at a time</u>.

6. Press <**Right Arrow**> four times. The cursor is on the "r" in "Excerpt."

7. Press <**Left Arrow**> twice. The cursor is on the "c" in "Excerpt."

Let's move a word at a time.

8. Hold <**Ctrl**> and press <**Right Arrow**>. The cursor is on the "f" in "from."

9. Hold <**Ctrl**> and press <**Right Arrow**>. The cursor is on the "t" in "the."

10. Hold <**Ctrl**> and press <**Left Arrow**> twice. The cursor is back to the "E" in "Excerpt."

Let's move along a line.

11. Press <**End**>. Cursor is at the end of the line, after the name "Franklin."

12. Press <**Home**>. The cursor is back to the "E" in "Excerpt."

Let's move among lines.

13. Press <**Down Arrow**> four times. The cursor is on the "s" in "seen", four lines down.

14. Press <**Up arrow**>. The cursor is on the "a" in "an", one line up.

15. Press <**PgDn**>. The cursor stays on "a" in "an", but the entire file moves (scrolls) up on the screen to reveal the next line at the bottom of the screen.

16. Press <**PgUp**>. The cursor stays on the "a" in "an", but the entire file scrolls down the screen to reveal the previous line at the top of the screen.

Let's move among sentences.

17. Hold <**Shift**> and <**Ctrl**> and press <**Right Arrow**>. The cursor moves to the end of the first sentence in the first paragraph.

18. Hold <**Shift**> and <**Ctrl**> and press <**Right Arrow**> three times. The cursor moves three sentences to the end of the paragraph.

19. Hold <**Shift**> and <**Ctrl**> and press <**Left Arrow**> three times. The Cursor moves to the end of the first sentence.

Let's <u>move among paragraphs</u>.

20. Hold **<Ctrl>** and press **<PgDn>**. The cursor is at the beginning of the second paragraph.

21. Hold **<Ctrl>** and press **<PgDn>** twice. The cursor is at the beginning of the last paragraph.

22. Hold **<Ctrl>** and press **<PgUp>** twice. The cursor is at the beginning of the second paragraph.

Let's <u>move from one end of the file to the other</u>.

23. Hold **<Alt>** and press **<White +>**. The cursor is at the beginning of the file.

24. Hold **<Alt>** and press **<White ->**. The cursor is at the end of the file.

25. Press **F1** then **F2** to quit PC-Write.

This guided activity is completed.

CHECKPOINT

Which key combination moves the cursor one sentence at a time?

_____

USING THE EDIT STATUS LINE

The term **edit** means to add, delete, or modify text, correct spelling, and make other changes to the text in a document. When a document is being edited, the line at the top of the screen is called the **edit status line**. It is shown in Figure 3-3. You can do the following from the edit status line.

To Bring Up the PC-Write Main Menus

- Press <Esc> The Esc Main Menu appears on the screen.
- Press <Esc> then <Alt> The Alt Main menu appears on the screen.
- Press <Esc> then <Shift> The Shift Main menu appears.
- Press <Esc> then <Ctrl> The Control Main menu appears on the screen.

Here is what happens on the screen:

Pressing a menu keys causes the associated menu to appear at the top of the screen. Each menu contains a series of PC-Write commands. Figure 3-7 shows the Esc main menu. See Appendix D for more information on the PC-Write menus.

Note: Pressing <Esc> in the edit mode may not consistently bring the Esc main menu to the screen. In such cases, press the <Home> key or press the <Up Arrow> or <Down Arrow> keys. Another main menu must already be on the screen for the <Home> and <Arrow> keys to successfully retrieve the Esc main menu.

```
F1:System/help  F3.Copy/mark   F5.Un-mark    F7.Paragraph   F9:Find-text
F2:Window/ruler F4.Delete/mark F6.Move/mark  F8.Lower/upper F10:Replace
```

FIGURE 3-7 THE ESC MAIN MENU

To Change to Overwrite Mode

■ Press <Scroll Lock>.

Here is what happens on the screen:

The cursor changes to about one-third its original thickness. The word "Push" at the top of the screen changes to "Over."

Any typing you now do will overwrite (erase) the material to the right of the cursor. To return to the pushright mode, press <Scroll Lock>. The cursor returns to its former thickness.

A thin cursor means overwrite (erase text) mode. A thick cursor means pushright (move existing text to the right) mode. Which mode to use is a choice you make. You will probably find it more convenient to operate mostly in pushright.

To Turn Automatic Word Wrap, and Automatic Reformatting, On and Off

Word wrap means that text reaching the right margin will automatically wrap around to the next line. Reformatting refers to keeping text aligned between the left and right margins.

■ Hold down <Shift> and press F7 until the mode you want appears on the edit status line.

Here is what happens on the screen:

Wrap+ is the normal mode. Text that reaches the right margin will automatically wrap around to the next line. Automatic reformatting of paragraphs (i.e aligning text between the margins) is off. When Wrap+ is active, F7 must be pressed to reformat a paragraph.

Pressing <Shift>-F7 changes the Edit line from "Wrap+" to "Para+." In this mode, word wrap is on and automatic reformatting of paragraphs is on.

Pressing <Shift>-F7 a second time changes the edit line to read "Wrap-." In this mode, word wrap and automatic reformatting of paragraphs is off. To reformat manually, press F7.

Pressing <Shift>-F7 a third time returns the edit status line to the Wrap+ mode.

Edit Line Entry	Meaning
Esc:Menu	Pressing <Esc> brings up the Esc Main menu
Push	Pushright mode is active
Wrap+	Automatic word wrap is active
Sp-	Spelling checker is off
(X)% Free	The amount of memory remaining
(Y)% Thru	How far into the document the cursor is
Edit "B:<file name>	Active file name on B drive disk

FIGURE 3-8 THE EDIT STATUS LINE SHOWING NORMAL OR DEFAULT SETTINGS

GUIDED ACTIVITY 3 CURSOR OPERATING MODES, AND AUTOMATIC REFORMATTING

This is the first guided activity in which you are asked to change text in a document. Similar activities appear throughout the rest of the text. It is possible that you may lose your position when performing an activity, or not have enough laboratory time to finish an activity, or simply want to repeat an activity. If you want to start a guided activity over again from the beginning, see "To Start All Over Again" in Unit 5, Saving and Printing a Document.

This guided activity demonstrates control of the cursor size, and the resultant affect on text entry. Automatic reformatting of paragraphs is also demonstrated

1. Get PC-Write ready (Ref. Figure 3-1).

2. Type **ED B:BF.DOC** and press **<Enter>**.

3. Press **<Esc>**. An excerpt from The Autobiography of Benjamin Franklin is on the screen. The cursor is in the upper left-hand corner of the file in column 1.

4. Press F2 to bring the ruler line to the screen. Type **L** at column 10, type **R** at column 72, and press **F2**.

5. Press **<Scroll Lock>** and notice that the cursor changes to about one-third of its original thickness.

6. Slowly press **<Scroll Lock>** five times in a row. Notice that the cursor changes thickness, and the word "Push" in the edit status line changes to "Over" and back again.

7. Verify that you are in the pushright mode (thick cursor).

8. Hold down **<Shift>** and press function Key **F7**. Notice that the edit status line now shows "Para+", indicating that automatic paragraph reformattingis on. This means that any changes made will be reformatted automatically within the paragraph margins.

9. Move the cursor to the beginning of the third paragraph, under the "T" in "Then", and press the **<Space Bar>** three times. Notice that the word "Then" has been pushed to the right, and that the paragraph has been automatically reformatted. As long as "Para+" is active, paragraphs will automatically reformat.

10. Move the cursor to the right and place it on the "S" in "Spectator." Type **SPECTATOR** and press <Space Bar> once. Notice that the new "SPECTATOR" pushed the old one to the right and that the paragraph was reformatted.

11. Delete the old "Spectator" with **<Del>**.

12. Press **<Home>** and delete the three spaces at the beginning of the paragraph.

13. Press F1 then F3 to save the changes made thus far.

14. Move the cursor to the "S" in "Spectator" in the first paragraph and press <Scroll Lock>. You are now in the overwrite mode. (Notice that as soon as you left paragraph three it reformatted automatically).

15. Type **SPECTATOR** to overwrite "Spectator."

16. Press **F1** then **F2**. Your changes are saved, PC-Write is exited, and the DOS prompt returns to the screen.

This activity is completed.

CHECKPOINT

How can PC-Write be set to reformat paragraphs automatically?

EDITING TEXT

There are two basic ways to edit text. You can add new text or delete existing text.

To Add Text

- Move the cursor to the desired location and, while in the pushright mode, key in the new text. Existing text on the right will be pushed to the right.
- Move the cursor to the desired location and, while in the overwrite mode, key in the new text. Existing text on the right will be overwritten (erased).

To Delete Text

In Pushright Mode

- Place the cursor at the beginning of the unwanted text and press <Del> until the unwanted text is erased. Any existing text on the right is pulled to the left.
- Place the cursor one space beyond the unwanted text and press <Backspace> until the unwanted text is erased. Any existing text on the right is pulled to the left.

In Overwrite Mode

- Place the cursor at the beginning of the unwanted text and press <Del> until the unwanted text is erased. Any existing text on the right is pulled to the left.
- Place the cursor one space beyond the unwanted text and press <Backspace> until the unwanted text is erased. Any existing text on the right stays put. Each erased character is replaced with a blank space.

In Pushright or Overwrite Mode

- To erase a word to the right of the cursor, press and hold <Ctrl>, and then press <Esc>.
- To erase a word to the left of the cursor, press and hold <Ctrl>, and then press <Backspace>.
- To erase a portion of a line from the cursor location to the end of the line, press and hold <Ctrl>, and then press <Enter>.
- To erase a word, line, or block of text, move the cursor to the beginning of the unwanted text and press F4. Move the cursor to the end of the unwanted text and press F4 again.

GUIDED ACTIVITY 4 ADDING AND DELETING TEXT,
AND MANUAL REFORMATTING

When you complete this guided activity, your screen should look like Figure 3-9.

1. Get PC-Write ready (Ref. Figure 3-1).

2. Type **ED B:POPUL.DOC**, press **<Enter>**, and press **<Esc>**. The "Population Census"
document is now on the screen.

3. Press **F2** to bring the ruler line to the screen. Type **L** at column 15, type **R** at column 65, and
press **F2**.

PART 1 ADDING TEXT

4. Place the cursor on the "F" at the beginning of paragraph 2, type **The first census was in the
late seventeenth century.** and press **<Space Bar>** twice. Notice that the existing text has
been pushed to the right and off the screen.

5. Press **F7** to manually reformat the paragraph.

6. Place the cursor on the "o" in "or" near the end of the second sentence in the third paragraph.
Type **visiting residence,** and press **<Space Bar>**.

7. Press **F7** to reformat the paragraph.

8. Press **<Scroll Lock>** to make overwrite active.

9. Place the cursor on the first "s" is "statistics" near the end of the third paragraph, and type
census results would be achieved.

PART 2 DELETING TEXT

1. Place the cursor on the space between "Representatives" and "among" near the end of paragraph one.

2. Press **<Del>** until "among the states." is deleted.

3. Type a period at the end of "Representatives"

Text can also be deleted with the space bar when the overwrite mode is on.

4. Verify that overwrite is active.

5. Place the cursor on the space between "statistics" and "on", near the end of paragraph 2.

6. Type **.** (Type a period.)

7. Hold down the space bar until "on other subjects." is deleted.

Text can also be deleted with the backspace key.

8. Press **<Scroll Lock>** to make pushright active.

9. Place the cursor on the <u>space</u> after "place," at the beginning of the second sentence in the third paragraph.

10. Press **<Backspace>** six times. Notice that the word "place" and a space is deleted.

11. Press **F7** to reformat the paragraph.

12. The backspace key also works in the overwrite mode, but an empty space is left where text has been deleted. Try it on some text in paragraph three. Then add back the text you delete.

PART 3: SPELLING CORRECTION

13. Make Overwrite active.

14. Place the cursor on the "d" in "consditution" at the beginning of paragraph one and Type **t** to correct the spelling.

15. Correct the spelling of "memebers" in the first paragraph, and "permamebt" in the second paragraph.

16. Change "if" to "of" and "it" to "It" in the the second paragraph.

17. Compare your screen with Figure 3-9. They should be the same.

18. Press **F1** then **F2**. Your changes are saved, PC-Write is exited, and the DOS prompt returns to the screen.

This activity is completed.

CHECKPOINT

How may paragraphs be reformatted when the Wrap+ mode is active?

Population Census

The constitution of the United States provides for
a census (counting) of the population within every
10-year period. This is done primarily to
establish a basis for apportionment of Members of
the House of Representatives.

The first census was in the late seventeenth
century. For over a century after the first census
in 1790, the census organization was a temporary
one. In 1902, the Bureau of the Census was
established. It is a permanent federal agency
responsible for counting the population and also
for compiling statistics.

In population censuses, each person is counted as
an inhabitant of his usual place of residence.
This is not necessarily his legal residence,
voting residence, visiting residence, or domicile.
But even if one of these were consistently used in
the census for everyone, substantially the same
census results would be achieved.

FIGURE 3-9 THE EDITED POPUL.DOC DOCUMENT,
THE RESULT OF GUIDED ACTIVITY 4

Application

1. Load the document EDITME.DOC. Set the margins at 10 and 65. Set automatic reformatting of Paragraphs on.

2. Insert this sentence between the first and second sentence in paragraph one: **All that changes when you enter college.**

3. Delete the word "rather" in the second sentence of paragraph two. Insert **for your actions** after the word "responsibility" in paragraph two. Insert **the benefit of** after the words "If you want" in the next to last sentence in paragraph two.

4. Set Wrap+ on. Place the cursor on the "T" in "There" at the beginning of the third paragraph, and add this sentence: **As far as a control system goes, forget it.** Reformat paragraph 3.

5. Type the following as paragraph four:

   You are now a free agent. The control has shifted. You are now in charge. You are now responsible for your learning. You are responsible for your academic success. You are solely responsible. You are a college student.

6. Correct all ten spelling errors and reformat as necessary.

7. Enter your name and date at the bottom of the document.

8. The printing of documents is discussed in Units 4 and 5. For those who can't wait, and want to print something out now, do the following:

   a) Press F1 then F2 to quit PC-Write.

   b) At the DOS prompt type **PR B:EDITME.DOC** and press **<Enter>**. If requested, type in a printer control file name.

   c) Verify that the printer is ready.

d) Press F10 twice.

Remove the document from the printer, frame it, and hang in on the wall next to your place of study.

REVIEW QUESTIONS

1. How do you get PC-Write ready to operate?

_____

_____

_____

2. What are the names of the four PC-Write main menus?

_____

_____

_____

_____

3. List the procedure for loading a document called EXAMPLE.DOC directly from the DOS prompt. Assume your computer is turned off and that the document file is on the disk in drive B. Use as many lines as you need.

_____

_____

_____

_____

_____

_____

_____

4. Repeat question 3, but assume you type only ED at the DOS prompt.

_____

_____

_____

_____

_____

_____

_____

_____

5. List the procedure for loading a document when another document is already in memory.

_____

_____

_____

_____

_____

_____

6. Does loading a file into memory remove it from the disk?

7. Indicate how the following keys move the cursor.

Key	Cursor moves
<Right Arrow>	_____
<Ctrl> and <Left Arrow>	_____
<End>	_____
<Home>	_____
<Down Arrow>	_____
<PgUp>	_____
<Shift> and <Ctrl> then <Right Arrow>	_____
<Ctrl> and <PgUp>	_____
<Shift> and <PgDn>	_____
<Alt> and <White + >	_____
<Alt> and <White ->	_____

8. Describe the functions that can be controlled through the edit status line.

_____

_____

_____

_____

_____

_____

_____

9. How are the PC-Write main menus brought to the screen?

_____

_____

_____

10. What does "Wrap+" on the edit status line signify?

_____

11. What does "Para+" on the edit status line signify?

_____

12. What does the lower case B next to the word Edit on the Edit Status line signify?

_____

13. What does pressing F1 then F2 accomplish when editing a document?

_____

DOCUMENTATION RESEARCH

Using the reference manual, find and record the page number for the general procedures listed below.

Page   General
Number   Procedure

_____ To Load a File From the DOS Prompt

_____ To Load a File When Another File is Already Loaded

_____ To Load a File From Within PC-Write

_____ To set temporary Left and Right Margins With the Ruler Line

_____ To Save and Continue Editing

_____ To Save and Quit PC-Write

_____ To Bring Up PC-Write's Main menus

_____ To Change to Overwrite Mode

_____ To Turn Automatic Word Wrap and Reformatting On and Off

_____ To Delete Text

_____ To Assign a Prefix

_____ To Display a Directory

UNIT

4

CREATING A NEW DOCUMENT

LEARNING OBJECTIVES

Upon completion of this unit you will know how to

1. create a new document file.

2. set permanent left and right margins.

3. check spelling.

4. insert the current date.

5. determine where page breaks will occur.

6. print a document.

UNIT OUTLINE

Learning Objectives

Unit Outline

Introduction

General Procedures

    Creating a Document File and Entering Text

        To Create a New Document

        To Set Permanent Left and Right Margins With the Ruler Line

        To Enter Text in a Document

        To Center Text on a Line

        To Set Page Breaks

        To Insert the Current Date

    Checking Spelling

        To Manually Check the Spelling of the Last Word Typed

        To Manually Correct the Spelling of a Word

        To Automatically Check the Spelling of a Word

    Printing a Document

        To Print While Editing a Document

        To Print From the DOS Prompt

Application B

Review Questions

Documentation Research

INTRODUCTION

In this unit you will create a document. You will use the ED (edit) command to load the PC-Write edit program and create a file name for your document. You will use the keyboard to enter text into your document.

Using the spelling checker, establishing where a page ends (called a page break), and printing a copy of your document are also covered.

GENERAL PROCEDURES

The general procedures covered in this unit fall into these categories:

Creating a Document File
Checking Spelling
Printing a Document

Whenever a file name is called for in the following examples, the example file name "Example.Fil" will be used.

CREATING A DOCUMENT FILE AND ENTERING TEXT

To Create A New Document

The general procedure for creating a new document is as follows:

Get PC-Write Ready.
Next to the A> prompt type ED B:EXAMPLE.FIL and press <Enter>.
Press F9.
Type your document.

Here is what happens on the screen:

The ED B:EXAMPLE.FIL command causes the Figure 4-1 screen to appear. Pressing the F9 function key causes the Figure 4-2 screen to appear. The screen is blank except for the edit status line at the top. You can now start typing your document.

```
File not found;  Esc to retype, or F9 to create "b:example.fil"

PC-Write (R). Version 2.71. Released on 24-Dec-86. Registration #013201
(C) Copyright 1983-1986 by Bob Wallace, Quicksoft. All Rights Reserved.
Shareware: Please help distribute PC-Write by sharing unmodified copies
of the diskettes in the U.S. and Canada.  Please don't copy the manual.
Please don't share copies elsewhere, to support our foreign publishers.
==> If you are using PC-Write, please buy a manual or a registered copy. <==

Compliments of:  Quicksoft  [this box available for your own message]

A registered copy provides you all the following benefits for only $89:
>  Printed hardbound copy of the full PC-Write manual and Quick Guide.
>  Current PC-Write diskette pair and your unique registration number.
>  PC-Write support service for one year:  includes telephone support,
    our quarterly newsletter, and two free update or source diskettes.
>  A $25 commission when someone registers and gives your reg. number.
>  Sincere thanks; your support helps us continue to improve PC-Write!

Hardbound manual $45, diskette pair $16. Quantity prices. Group license.
When you register, give registration #number above, to credit its owner.
PO, COD, Rush: add $5. Overseas add $20. WA orders add 7.9%. Visa/MC ok.
Quicksoft, Inc.  206/282-0452.  219 First North #224, Seattle, WA 98109.
```

FIGURE 4-1 THE PC-Write "HELLO" SCREEN WHEN CREATING A NEW FILE (EXAMPLE.FIL) BY TYPING ED B:EXAMPLE.FIL AT THE DOS PROMPT

```
Esc:MenuPush Wrap+Sp- 99% Free.  0% Thru.  Read "b:example.fil"

        [The rest of the screen is blank]
```

FIGURE 4-2 THE SCREEN AFTER PRESSING FUNCTION KEY F9 PER THE TOP LINE SHOWN IN FIGURE 4-1

To Set Permanent Left and Right Margins With the Ruler Line

Left and right paragraph margins should be set before you begin typing. This action will assure that your document conforms to whatever page layout you have in mind, and will help avoid extensive reformatting at a later date. Permanent margins become a permanent part of the document file because the ruler line is embedded in the document and saved with the document text. A permanent ruler line is shown in Figure 4-3.

- Create a document file or bring a document file to the screen.
- Move the cursor to the top of the screen.

■ Press F2. The default ruler line appears along with this ruler line menu:

Esc F1:Help F2.Clear F3:To-file F4.Insert F5.Default F6:From-file Grey-

■ Move the cursor to the column where you want the left margin to be and type a capital L.
■ Move the cursor to the column where you want the right margin to be and type a capital R.
■ Press F4 to insert the ruler line settings and its new margins in the document.
■ Press F2 to remove the default line. To see the permanent ruler line, press <Down Arrow>.
■ Start or continue typing.

Multiple ruler lines with different margin settings can be permanently inserted anywhere in a document. Remember that a ruler line inserted in a document affects all the material typed below it.

Permanent ruler lines remain highlighted in the file so they are easy to see. To display an embedded ruler line, press F2 to bring up the default ruler line. Then press <Grey+> to display the next embedded ruler line or press <Grey-> to display the prior embedded ruler line. PC-Write does not jump to the next or previous ruler line in the text. It displays the next or previous ruler line in the same space occupied by the default ruler line.

The edit program recognizes an embedded ruler line because the ruler line starts with a guide line font character. The guide line character is a small circle with an attached, upward-pointing arrow. See Figure 4-3. Embedded ruler lines are actually regular text characters and therefore such lines can be editied, copied, moved, or deleted just like any other text. However, do not delete the guide line font character since it signifies an embedded ruler line to the edit program.

♂---------L--+-T--2----T----3--T-+----4T---+---T5----+-T--6----T----7-R-------r

FIGURE 4-3 AN EMBEDDED RULER LINE WITH MARGINS AT COLUMNS 10 AND 72

To Enter Text in a Document

The general procedure for typing a document is as follows:

■ The <Caps Lock> key should be off. When it is on, all the letters you type will appear in upper case. You can tell if the <Caps Lock> key is on by looking for "cap" on the left side of the edit status line line.

- The <Num Lock> key should be off. When it is on, the numeric keypad (on the right side of the keyboard) provides numbers only. The cursor control keys are not usable. You can tell if the <Num Lock> key is on by looking for "num" on the left side of the top line.
- Word wrap should be on. Look for "Wrap+" on the Edit Status line.

To Center Existing Text on a Line

- Move cursor to line to be centered.
- Press <Esc> to bring up the Esc main menu.
- Press <Shift> to bring up the Shift main menu.
- Press F8 or highlight "Center" and press <Enter>.

OR

- Move cursor to the line to be centered.
- Press <Shift>-F8.

CHECKING SPELLING

PC-Write contains a 50,000 word list against which it checks the spelling of the words you type. If a word you type is not in the word list, its spelling cannot be checked. However, you can create a separate word list for checking words that you use but that are not in the regular 50,000-word list.

PC-Write cannot perform a global spelling check. This means you cannot type a whole document and ask the spelling checker to check spelling. You can manually check one word at a time, or you can have PC-Write automatically check spelling as you type.

Figure 4-4 shows the spelling checker menu.

```
Esc  F1  F2.Check  F3:Guess  F4:Add-word  F5:Load-List  F6:Save-List  F7.Auto+  Grey+
```

FIGURE 4-4 THE SPELLING CHECKER MENU

To Manually Check the Spelling of the Last Word Typed

- Move the cursor anywhere on the word to be checked, or to the space following the word.
- Press <Alt>-F2.
- Press F2.

Here is what happens on the screen:

Pressing <Alt>-F2 loads the spelling checker program and brings the spelling checker menu (Figure 4-4) to the screen. These are the menu choices:

Esc: Cancels spelling menu.

F1: Displays help topics.

F2: Checks if last word typed is in dictionary.

F3: Guesses at correct spelling for last word checked.

F4: Adds this word to user list in memory.

F5: Loads user word list from disk into memory.

F6: Saves user word list now in memory to disk.

F7: Turns automatic spell checker (checks each word typed) on+ or off-.

Grey: Searches forward (Grey+) or backward (Grey-) for word not in dictionary.

When F2 is pressed, the spelling checker searches for the word in the dictionary. If the word is found this message appears on the screen: **Found in master word list: "word"**. If this message appears, you can assume the word is correctly spelled.

If the word is not found this message appears on the screen: **Not found in word list:** If this message appears it means that

a) the word is misspelled

OR,

b) The word is spelled correctly, but is not in the 50,000-word dictionary.

If you believe the word is misspelled, you can correct it as shown below. If you know it is spelled correctly, you can add it to your own word list by pressing F4.

To Manually Correct the Spelling of a Word

■ move cursor anywhere on word, or to space following word.
■ Press <Alt>-F2.

- Press F2.
- Press F3.
- Press F10.
- Press <Esc>.

Here is what happens on the screen:

Pressing <Alt>-F2 loads the spelling checker program and brings the spelling checker menu (Figure 4-4) to the screen.

When F2 is pressed, the spelling checker searches for the word in the dictionary. If the word is found, this message is displayed: **Found in master word list: "word"**. If the word is not found, this messsage is displayed: **Not found in word list (Esc F3:Guess F4:Add etc): "word"**

Presssing F3 brings this menu to the screen: **Esc: F3.Guess F10.Replace "{existing word}" with "{suggested word}"** "Suggested word" represents a guess on PC-Write's part. Keep pressing F3 until a suitable substitute appears on the top line.

When a suitable substitute appears, press F10. The word is automatically corrected in your document.

If you get the message **Cannot guess word [press any key]** it means that PC-Write cannot help you spell the word correctly and you must check the spelling with a regular printed dictionary.

To Automatically Check the Spelling of a Word

- Press <Alt>-F2.
- Press F7.
- Start typing.

Here is what happens on the screen:

Pressing <Alt>-F2 loads the spelling checker program and brings the spelling menu to the screen.

Pressing F7 invokes the automatic spelling checker, and the edit status line returns to the screen. The status line will show **Sp+**.

Start typing. When you type a word that is NOT in the PC-Write dictionary, PC-Write will will beep at you. You can then attempt to correct the spelling as described above.

To turn off the automatic spelling check feature, press <Alt>-F2 and then press F7. The status line will show **Sp-**.

You will probably find that the automatic mode is the best way to use the spelling checker.

To Insert the Current Date

PC-Write has a feature which allows you to automatically insert the current date anywhere in your document. Proceed as follows:

- Move the cursor to where you want the current date inserted.
- Press <Alt>-F4.
- Press F5.

Here is what happens on the screen.

Pressing <Alt>-F4 brings the "Misc-Stuff" menu to the screen. One of the menu items is **F5-Date-ins. Pressing F5 inserts the date at the cursor in this format: January 15, 1990.**

The correct date will appear only if you have typed in the current date during the process of bringing the DOS prompt to the screen.

PRINTING A DOCUMENT

Before printing, make sure you have placed page breaks in the document. Otherwise, the page breaks may appear in awkward locations. To print a document, use either of the following two procedures.

To Print While Editing a Document

When a document is already loaded in memory, and on the screen, proceed as follows:

- Press F1 to bring up the System/help menu.
- Press F7 to select "Print".
- Press <Enter> to accept the current file name.
- Verify that the printer is ready.
- Press F10 to confirm the printer is ready.
- Press F10 to start printing.

Note: If you configured PC-Write for only one printer, then you have a PR.DEF printer control file on your working disk and the print sequence will work as shown above. If you configured PC-Write to work with more than one printer, then you do not have a PR.DEF printer control file. In such cases, after you press <Enter> to accept the current file name, you will be asked to type in the name of a printer control file you created. After doing so, press <Enter>.

To Print From the DOS Prompt

- Get PC-Write ready.
- Type PR B:<filename>
- Verify that the printer is ready.
- Press F10 twice.

See Unit 5, Saving and Printing, for additional material on printing a document.

GUIDED ACTIVITY 1 CREATING A DOCUMENT

1. Get PC-Write ready.

2. Type **ED B:BALANCE.DOC**

3. Press **F9**.

4. Move the cursor to the top of the ruler line and embed a permanent ruler line with margins at columns 13 and 72. Use the procedure described earlier in this unit.

5. Press **<Alt>-F2** and then press **F7** to activate the automatic spelling checker.

6. Type all the following material that appears in boldface. Leave six blank lines at the top of the page.

**A DESCRIPTION OF A
BALANCE SHEET**

**Prepared by: (type your name here)
(insert the current date here)**

A balance sheet shows the result of operating a company over a given period of time. The time period is usually one year. A balance sheet has three parts: assets, liabilities, and capital.

Assets are valuable things owned by the company. Liabilities are debts owed by the company to banks and claims against it by suppliers (trade creditors). Capital is the amount of the company's assets (after paying all liabilities) that would be divided among owners if the company were sold or went out of business.

The balance sheet is important because it shows how well a company is operating. It shows the proportion of all the company's assets owned by or owed to its trade creditors, banks, and owners. If the proportion owned by owners increases, the company is doing well.

Examples of assets are:

 - Bank accounts

 - Accounts payable (amounts due from customers)

 - Inventories

 - Property, plant, and equipment

 - Copyrights and patents

Examples of liabilities are:

 - Accounts payable (amounts owed to trade creditors)

 - Insurance, retirement plans, other

 - Taxes payable

 - Short-term loans

 - Long-term loans

Examples of capital are:

 - Owners' investment

 - Retained earnings

A balance sheet is called a balance sheet because when properly constructed, the addition of liabilities to capital will equal--or balance--the assets (i.e Assets = Liabilities + Capital).

7. Press **F1** to bring up the System/Help menu.

8. Press **F7** to select Print.

9. Press **<Enter>** and notice you are asked to verify that the printer is ready.

10. Verify that the printer is ready and the paper is positioned to start printing at the top of the page. Press **F10**.

11. Notice that the print menu appears.

12. Press **F10** to print the document from beginning to end.

13. Notice that when printing is completed, the edit program is automatically loaded back into memory and the edit status line returns to the screen.

14. Press **F1** then **F2** to quit PC-Write.

This guided activity is completed.

Checkpoint

How should the <Num Lock> and <Caps Lock> keys be set when entering text in a document?

GUIDED ACTIVITY 2 CHECKING SPELLING

1. Bring the file BALANCE.DOC to the screen. If you have not created this document, refer to Guided Activity 1 in this unit.

2. Verify that a permanent ruler line (with margins at columns 13 and 72) is present.

3. The document contains seven paragraphs. Move to each paragraph and purposely misspell at least one word in each paragraph.

4. Refer to the general spelling check procedure described earlier in this unit. Check the spelling using the following methods:

   a) manually check the spelling of the last word typed.

   b) manually correct the spelling of a word.

   c) automatically check the spelling of a word.

Checkpoint

What key combination invokes the spelling checker?

Checkpoint

Explain why a word not found by the spelling checker does not necessarily mean that the word is misspelled.

To Set Page Breaks

Documents are usually printed on paper eleven inches long with six lines per inch (sixty-six lines per page; the top and bottom two lines are left blank). PC-Write assumes this convention as its normal way of operating. This means that if your document is longer than one page, PC-Write will print the first sixty-six lines of your document on the first page and then start a new page.

Sometimes the default setting of sixty-six lines produces awkward results. For example, if the last line on a page were a topic heading, you would want that line shifted to the top of the next page. If a table started at the bottom of one page and finished at the top of another, you would want the whole table to appear on the next page.

You can avoid awkward page breaks, because PC-Write allows you to override the default setting of sixty-six lines per page. You can start a new page wherever you want. Page breaks should be inserted only after you have completed typing all the text. The procedure for establishing page breaks is as follows:

- Type your document.
- Move to the top of your document by holding down <Alt> and pressing <White + >.
- Hold down <Alt> and press F7. The screen now displays a symbol in the left margin which shows where a new page will start. The symbol is a circle with crossed lines on the bottom. Press the down arrow key to see any remaining symbols in the document. Each symbol represents the beginning of a new page. If the symbol locations are acceptable, the document may be printed..

If the page breaks are not acceptable to you, do the following:

- Delete the offending page break symbol by using the delete key.
- Move the cursor to the left margin of the line you want at the top of a page. NOTE: The line you move to must be **above** the page break you have just deleted.

- Hold down <Alt>-<Shift> and press the letter T. You have inserted a page break symbol where you want it.
- Now Press <Alt>-F7 to repage your document. All existing page breaks following the one you have just inserted are automatically reset.
- Determine if the new page break locations are acceptable and repage if necessary.

When the document is printed, a new page will begin where the page break symbols appear. If you later add new text or blank lines, you will have to repage the document and verify that the page breaks appear where you want them.

Note: Pressing <Alt>-T inserts a "hard" page break, denoted by two symbols in the left margin. Such page breaks are not reset by repaging. They remain until removed with the delete key.

GUIDED ACTIVITY 3   SETTING PAGE BREAKS

1. Bring the file BALANCE.DOC to the screen. If you have not created this document, refer to Guided Activity 1 in this unit.

2. Verify that a permanent ruler line (with margins at columns 13 and 72) is present.

3. Verify that there are ten blank lines at the top of the document.

4. Press **<Alt>-<White+>** to bring the cursor to the top left corner of the document.

5. Press **<Alt>-F7** to page the document. Notice that the page break appears between the lines "Owners' investment" and "Retained earnings." Since this is an awkward break, we will reset it.

6. Remove the page break with **<Delete>**.

7. Move the cursor to the left margin of the line that reads "Examples of capital are" and then press **<Alt>-<Shift>** and **T** to insert a new page break.

8. Print the document. Notice that the second page starts with the line "Examples of capital are." This is where you inserted the page break.

This activity is completed.

Checkpoint

If you do not specify where you want page breaks, where are they placed? Why could this prove awkward?

Application

One format that personal data sheets (resumes) follow is:

> Name, address, and telephone number at the top of the page, followed by

> I Educational Background
> (List dates, school names, major subjects. List most recent dates first.)

> II Work Experience
> (List dates, company names, job title, responsibilities. List most recent dates first.)

> III Extra-curricular activities
> (List clubs, community organizations, other activities.)

> IV References

Using this pattern, prepare your one-page personal data sheet. Try to attain the spacing and "look" of the example personal data sheet shown in Appendix C, Typical Documents. It is not necessary to underline or boldface (make text appear darker) any of the the text.

Print the personal data sheet twice, once while in the edit mode and once from the DOS prompt.

REVIEW QUESTIONS

1. Show the command for creating a document from the DOS prompt.

_____

2. Where is your document stored during editing?

_____

3. What should be the settings on the edit status line when entering text in a document?

_____

_____

4. What is the command sequence for centering text on a line?

_____

_____

_____

5. How is the spelling checker made active?

_____

6. List the entries on the spelling checker menu.

_____

_____

_____

_____

_____

_____

_____

_____

_____

7. List the procedure for manually checking the spelling of a word.

_____

_____

_____

_____

_____

_____

_____

8. How is automatic spelling checker made active?

_____

9. How is the current date inserted in a document?

_____

10. List the procedure for paging a document.

_____

_____

_____

_____

_____

_____

11. List the procedure for printing a document while editing.

_____

_____

_____

_____

_____

_____

_____

12. List the procedure for printing a document from the DOS prompt.

_____

_____

_____

_____

_____

_____

_____

13. Why are the column number positions not the same on the default (F2) ruler line and a permanent (F4) ruler line?

_____

_____

_____

_____

DOCUMENTATION RESEARCH

Consult the PC-Write manual on the topic of backup files and provide the following information.

1. What is the significance of "&" in a file name extension?

_____

2. What is the significance of "%" in a file name extension?

UNIT

5

SAVING AND PRINTING A DOCUMENT

LEARNING OBJECTIVES

Upon completion of this unit you should know how to

1. save a document with a different file name.

2. avoid saving changes and so you can begin editing all over again.

3. Use dot commands to print a document with double line spacing.

4. Use dot commands to print a document with keyboard Input.

UNIT OUTLINE

INTRODUCTION

Unit 3 covered the fundamentals of saving a document and Unit 4 covered the fundamentals of printing a document. This unit contains additional material on saving and printing. This unit also introduces the dot line command. A dot line command allows one to use certain PC-Write functions by inserting commands directly in the document text, or by inserting commands directly from the keyboard.

GENERAL PROCEDURES

SAVING A DOCUMENT

There are actually several ways to save a document. In fact, if you look closely at the System/Help menu (Figure 5-1), you will discover that it is mainly a Save menu.

Esc F1:Help F2.Exit F3.Save F4.Command F5:Name F6:File F7:Print F8:Dir   F9:Unsave

FIGURE 5-1 THE SYSTEM/HELP MENU

Here is what each command accomplishes:

F1: Brings Help menu to the screen.

F2: Saves document, quits PC-Write, returns to DOS prompt.

F3: Saves document, remains in edit mode.

F4: Saves document, temporarily exits to DOS prompt.

F5: Saves document under new file name.

F6: Saves document; can then load or create another document.

F7: Saves document; can then print a document.

F8: Lists directory of document file names on selected disk.

F9: Cancels (makes inoperative) F2, F4, F6, F7 save operations.

Each menu option can be invoked by pressing the corresponding function key or by pointing to a selection via the <Right Arrow> or <Left Arrow> and pressing <Enter>.

The save procedures presented in Unit 3 are shown here again for purposes of completeness and handy reference.

To Save and Continue Editing

- Press F1 to bring up the Figure 5-1 System/Help menu.
- Press F3 to select Save.

The document is saved and you can continue editing.

Here is what happens on the screen:

When F1 is pressed the System/Help menu appears at the top of the screen as shown in Figure 5-1. When you press F3 you are actually selecting Save from the menu.

Save your document periodically, perhaps every twenty minutes. This will guard against losing large portions of your text in the event a computer failure or power outage occurs. It's as easy as F1-F3.

To Save and Quit

- Press F1
- Press F2

The document is saved and the DOS prompt appears on the screen.

To Quit Without Saving

You may have occasion to alter and print a document, but don't want the changes to be a permanent part of the file. Or you may start to make changes, determine you don't want them, and decide to quit PC-Write. In such cases, proceed as follows:

- Press F1 to bring up the System/Help menu.
- Press F9 to select "Unsave."
- Press F2 to quit PC-Write.

To Save a Document With a Different File Name

While you may have brought a document to the screen under one file name, you may want to save it under a different file name. This is useful when you want to a) change the name of a file, b) experiment with changes (but don't want them in your original file), c) create another file with the same text, or d) backup a file while editing.

- Press F1.
- Press F5.
- Type in the new file name.
- Press <Enter>.
- Press F1.
- Press F3.

Here is what happens on the screen:

When you press F1, the System menu appears on the screen. Pressing "F5:Name" from the System menu causes this message to appear:

> Name to use for saving (<Esc>:cancel F8:Dir): "b:sample.fil"

The cursor is under the "b" indicating the B drive is active. You now type in the new file name. The name you type renames the file in <u>memory</u>. It does not rename the file on disk. When you issue the F1-F3 save command, the file is saved to disk using the new file name you typed in.

If you type a file name that already exists, this message appears:

> File found; press Esc to cancel, F9 to replace "b:sample.fi2"

Pressing <Esc> allows you to try again with a new file name. Pressing F9 means you will use the name of an existing disk file. The next time you issue a save command, the original contents of that disk file (whose name you just used for the file in memory) will be lost.

To Start All Over Again

When making changes in a document you may lose track of where you are in the change process, and wish for a chance to start over again.

- Press F1.
- Press F9.
- Press F6.
- Press <Enter>.

■ Start again.

Here is what happens on the screen:

Pressing F1 brings up the System menu (see Figure 5-1). One of the commands on this menu is F9-Unsave. Pressing F9 changes the right side of the System menu from F9-Unsave to [Unsave].

Pressing F6 causes the top line to look like this:

> Name of file to switch to (Esc to cancel): "sample.fil"

Sample.fil is the name of the file you made changes to but do not want to save. Pressing <Enter> causes the edit program to load (i.e. switch to) the original version of the file, which is on the disk in its original, unchanged state. Loading the original version of the file back into memory wipes the changed version out of memory. You can now begin again.

GUIDED ACTIVITY 1   SAVING WITH A DIFFERENT FILE NAME

1. Get PC-Write ready.

2. Type **ED B:BF.DOC**, press **<Enter>**, and press **<Esc>**.

3. Press **F1** to bring up the System menu.

4. Press **F5**. The top line now reads: "Name to use for saving (<Esc>;cancel F8:Dir): 'B:BF.DOC'"

5. Notice that the cursor is under the first B. We want to use a new file name, so we will type in the new name.

6. Type **B:FRANKLIN.BIO** and press **<Enter>**. The edit status line returns.

7. Press **F1** then **F3**. The document is saved under the new file name. Any changes now made to the document will be saved under the new name.

8. Press **F1** then **F2** to quit PC-Write.

This activity is completed.

Checkpoint

When saving with a different file name, what happens when you type in a file name that already exists?

PRINTING A DOCUMENT

The print menu (Figure 5-2) provides options other than just printing out a copy of a document.

```
F1.Help-screen F3.Finished   F5:Input-end F7:Repeat-pages F9.Page-stop
F2.Exit-to-DOS F4.DOS-command F6:User-input F8:Skip-pages   F10.Continuous
```

FIGURE 5-2 THE PRINT MENU

Here is what each command accomplishes:

F2: Exits to DOS.

F3: Exits to DOS or edit program, whichever started printing.

F4: Exits to DOS; return by typing "Exit" at the DOS prompt.

F5: Stops printing the current input file.

F6: Enters text from the keyboard.

F7: Repeats a page or prints multiple copies.

F8: Skips over specified pages prior to printing.

F9: Prints current page.

F10: Prints continuously; <Esc> stops printing.

Each menu option can be invoked by pressing the corresponding function key or by pointing to a selection via the <Right Arrow> or <Left Arrow> and pressing <Enter>.

The print procedures presented in Unit 4 are shown here again for purposes of completeness and handy reference.

To Print While Editing a Document

When a document is already loaded in memory, and on the screen, proceed as follows:

- Press F1 to bring up the System/Help menu.
- Press F7 to select "Print".
- Press <Enter> to accept the current file name.
- Verify that the printer is ready.
- Press F10 to confirm the printer is ready.
- Press F10 to start printing.

Note: If you configured PC-Write for only one printer, then you have a PR.DEF printer control file on your working disk and the print sequence will work as shown above. If you configured PC-Write to work with more than one printer, then you do not have a PR.DEF printer control file. In such cases, after you press <Enter> to accept the current file name, you will be asked to type in the name of a printer control file you created. After doing so, press <Enter>.

Here is what happens on the screen:

When you press F1 the System menu appears. Pressing F7:Print from the System menu causes the file to be saved and this menu to appear:

        File to print (Esc:cancel F8:dir): "b:Sample.Fil"

Sample.Fil is the name of the file in memory. To tell PC-Write to print the file in memory, press <Enter>.

Pressing <Enter> causes this menu to appear:

        Esc:Exit F9: Print to a File F10:Printer is Ready

Check that the printer is on-line and that the paper is positioned to start printing at the top of the page. Pressing F10 brings up the print menu shown in Figure 5-2.

One of the print menu entries is "F10:Continuous." Pressing F10 causes the document to be printed.

To Print a Document From the DOS Prompt

- Get PC-Write ready.
- Type PR B:<filename> and press <Enter>. (PR is the name of PC-Write's print program.)

■ Verify that the printer is ready.
■ Press F10.
■ Press F10.

Note: If you configured PC-Write for only one printer, then you have a PR.DEF printer control file on your working disk and the print sequence will work as shown above. If you configured PC-Write to work with more than one printer, then you do not have a PR.DEF printer control file. In such cases, after you type "PR B:Sample.fil" and press <Enter>, you will be asked to type in the name of a printer control file you created. After doing so, press <Enter>. After you press <Enter>, either a) or b) will occur.

a) If you do not have a PR.DEF printer control file, typing PR B:Sample.fil and pressing enter causes this message to appear:

Print control file name (Esc:exit Enter:none): ""

You now type in the name of a printer control file and press <Enter>. Upon doing so, the message shown immediately below will appear.

b) If you do have a PR.EXE file, typing PR B:Sample.fil and pressing <Enter> causes this message to appear:

Esc:Exit F9:Print to a file F10:Printer is ready

Pressing F10 causes the Figure 5-2 Print Menu to Appear.
Pressing F10 again prints the document.

USING DOT COMMANDS TO PRINT A DOCUMENT FROM THE EDIT PROGRAM

A dot command is a line of text placed in the document to direct PC- Write to perform some function. Since the line of text is preceded by a special character followed by a dot (a period), the PC-Write print program does not treat it as a regular line of text. It treats the line as a command.

The special character is entered by holding down <Alt> and pressing <G>. The resultant character, called a a guide line font character, instructs PC-Write to perform whatever function appears on the rest of the dot line. The guide line font character is a small circle with an attached, upward-pointing arrow. It is shown at the beginning of the first line in Figure 5-3.

In this section we will discuss the use of dot lines to print a document with double line spacing and the use of dot lines to print a document with keyboard input.

To Print a Double-Spaced Document Using Embedded Dot Commands

PC-Write normally prints documents single spaced, but you can change the spacing to whatever is desired. Line spacing can be set by inserting a dot line command in the document. The dot line takes the form **<guide line font character>.M:N** where N, which must be a whole number, represents the number of blank lines between each line of text. Figure 5-3 shows a sample screen with a dot line for double spacing.

⌐**.M:2**
   Although this text is single spaced on the screen, the dot
   line above will cause it to print double spaced. If the
   number two were changed to a three, then these lines would
   print triple spaced.   Dot lines must be placed on a blank
   line. Each dot line command must appear on a separate line.
   Each dot line must be preceded by the guide line font
   character. The guide line font character is entered by
   holding down <Alt> and pressing <G>.

**FIGURE 5-3 A SAMPLE SCREEN WITH A DOT LINE TO PRODUCE A DOCUMENT
              WITH DOUBLE LINE SPACING**

To enter the dot line shown in Figure 5-3, proceed as follows:

- Move the cursor to column one, or the left margin, at the top of the document. If the first line is occupied by text, insert a blank line above the text. Dot lines must be entered on a blank line since a dot line entered on a text line will cause the print program to ignore that text. Enter only one dot line command per line.
- Enter the guide line font character by holding down <Alt> and pressing the letter <G>.
- Type a dot (a period), the letter M, a colon, and the number two.
- Print the document.

A dot line placed at the beginning of a document will affect the whole document. A dot line placed elsewhere in the document will affect the text immediately below it. Dot lines are saved along with the rest of the document. They can be deleted with <Del>.

GUIDED ACTIVITY 2 PRINTING WITH DOUBLE LINE SPACING

1. Load the file POPUL.DOC

2. Move the cursor to line one, column one. If the first line is occupied by text, insert a blank line.

3. Type the dot line shown at the top of Figure 5-3. Make sure to start the line with the guide line font character.

4. Print the document.

5. Remove the document from the printer and verify that a double space appears between each line of text.

6. Quit PC-Write.

This guided activity is completed.

Checkpoint

What would happen if the guide line font character were not typed at the beginning of a dot line?

To Print a Double-Spaced Document Using Dot Commands and Keyboard Input

Keyboard input is an alternative to embedding dot lines directly in the document.

- Press F1 to bring up the System/Help menu.
- Press F7 to select "Print".
- Press <Enter> to accept the current file name.
- Verify that the printer is ready.
- Press F10 to confirm the printer is ready.
- Press F6 to select "User-input." This message appears:

Will take user input lines when printing starts [press any key]

- Press F10 to print continuously. You are prompted with " "
- Type the dot line shown at the top of Figure 5-3.
- Press <Enter>.
- Press <Esc> to print the document.

GUIDED ACTIVITY 3 TRIPLE-SPACED PRINTING WITH KEYBOARD INPUT

1. Load the file BF.DOC.

2. Follow the procedure given under "To Print a Double-Spaced Document Using Dot Commands and Keyboard Input." When you are prompted with " ", type the dot line shown the top of Figure 5-3, substituting the number three for the number two.

3. After typing the dot line, remember to press <Enter>, then <Esc>.

4. Remove the document from the printer and verify that a triple space appears between each line of text.

5. Quit PC-Write.

This guided activity is completed.

Checkpoint

Why did the document not print immediately after F10 was pressed a second time?

_____

USING DOT COMMANDS TO PRINT A DOCUMENT FROM THE DOS PROMPT

- Type PR at the DOS prompt and press <Enter>.
- Verify that the printer is ready and press F10. The Print Menu is now on the screen.
- Press F10 to print continuously.
- The top of the screen now shows the " " prompt along with this message:

    Enter input text line or guide line in line above. Press Enter at end of line.
    Press F1 for Help screen. Press Esc after all lines entered to end input file.

- Type in the desired dot line commands. Precede each dot line with the <Alt>-<G> guide line font character. Press <Enter> at the end of each dot line.

    Note: One of the dot lines must be of the form **.T:B:SAMPLE.FIL**. A **.T:** dot line is the command to print a particular file.

- When all dot lines have been entered, Press <Esc> to print the document.

Application

The file FILLBAL.DOC contains a document with six sentences and nine areas filled with asterisks. The asterisks are to be replaced with words chosen from this list:

    valuable
    company (used twice)
    year
    time
    sold
    amount
    balance
    owners'

The document will then be printed using certain dot line commands entered through the keyboard.

1. Load the file and set the margins at 5 and 60.

2. Give the document a centered title, replace the asterisks with the words listed above, and make the last three sentences a separate paragraph. Leave a double space between paragraphs. Reformat as necessary. Leave ten blank lines after the second paragraph, and add your name and current date near the bottom of the page.

3. Quit PC-Write. Type **PR** at the DOS prompt and press **<Enter>**.

4. Verify that the printer is ready and press F10. The Print Menu is now on the screen. Press F10 to select "Continuous."

5. The top of the screen now shows the " " prompt. Type in the following individual dot lines. Precede each with the <Alt>-<G> guide line font character.

.M:2 and press **<Enter>**
> [This will double space the document.]

.X:10 and press **<Enter>**
> [This will move the printed text ten spaces to the right.]

.F: and press **<Enter>**
> [This will leave a blank line at the foot of the text.]

.F;...$$$... and press **<Enter>**
> [This will print a centered page number at the foot of the page.]

.T:B:FILLBAL.DOC and press **<Enter>**
> [This tells the print program which file to print.]

6. Press **<Esc>** to print the document.

7. Remove the document from the printer and verify that all the dot line commands have been carried out.

REVIEW QUESTIONS

1. What is the difference between saving and quitting, and quitting without saving?

_____

_____

_____

2. List the procedure for saving a document with a different file name.

_____

_____

_____

_____

_____

_____

3. This unit discusses two procedures for printing a document from the DOS prompt. Choose one of the procedures and list the steps below.

_____

_____

_____

_____

_____

_____

_____

4. What does a dot line represent ?

_____

_____

5. Draw a picture of the guide line font character here _____ .

6. Which key combination will cause the guide line font character to appear on the screen?

_____

7. Why must a dot line command appear on a line by itself?

_____

_____

8. Show the dot line command to print a document with triple spacing.

_____

9. List the functions that can be performed from the System menu.

_____

_____

_____

_____

_____

_____

_____

_____

_____

DOCUMENTATION RESEARCH

Consult the PC-Write manual on the topic of guide line dot commands and determine what each of the following commands accomplishes.

.N:<number>   _____

.DD   _____

.DB   _____

.L:<length>   _____

.T:filename   _____

2 INTERMEDIATE WORD PROCESSING OPERATIONS

Unit 6 discusses how to format text with the ruler line; the use of the ED.DEF edit control file to control margins and store date, time, and save functions; printing page numbers; and creating page headers, footers, and footnotes.

Unit 7 shows how to copy text from one part of a document to another, copy text from one document to another document, create a new file with text copied from another file, and move text within a document.

Unit 8 discusses how to find text so it may be changed or replaced, how to display the current location of the cursor, how to jump to another part of a document, and how to set a bookmark.

Unit 9 shows how to enhance the appearance of text through underlining, boldfacing, enlarging, reducing, and enclosing. In order to reproduce many of the enhancements in this unit, a printer which recognizes the IBM character set must be used. Printers which do not recognize the IBM character set will produce unpredictable results.

UNIT

6 TEXT AND PAGE FORMATTING

LEARNING OBJECTIVES

Upon completion of this unit you should know how to

1. use the ruler line to set different left and right margins in the same document, set paragraph margins, justify text, and set tab stops.

2. use the ED.DEF file to permanently change the default ruler line.

3. automatically insert the time and date.

4. be reminded to save your file.

5. create headers, footers, and print page numbers.

6. create footnotes.

UNIT OUTLINE

INTRODUCTION

This unit discusses how to format text through use of the ruler line, and the use of the ED.DEF edit control file to control margins and store date, time, and save functions. This Unit also discusses how to format pages with headers, footers, page numbers, and footnotes.

RULER LINE FUNDAMENTALS AND THE ED.DEF EDIT CONTROL FILE

When you created your PC-Write working disk (the disk you normally put in drive A), an edit control file was automatically placed on the disk. This file (named ED.DEF) contains a **ruler line** which controls the margins of the documents you type. It is called the **default** or **normal** ruler line. The default ruler line is shown in Figure 6-1.

```
L---+---T1----+-T--2-/\/\/\/\-T5----+-T--6----T----7--T-+--R
(1)                                                       (78)
```

FIGURE 6-1 THE DEFAULT RULER LINE SHOWING THE MARGINS SET AT COLUMNS 1 AND 78

The default ruler line has the left margin set at column 1--notice the capital L on the left side of the line in Figure 6-1. The right margin is set at column 78. The capital Ts in the ruler line represent tab stops. The numbers (multiplied by ten) represent column locations. When PC-Write is in the edit mode, you can see this ruler line by pressing function key F2.

When you create a new document file by using **ED B:(filename)**, the default ruler line shown in Figure 6-1 is automatically made part of your new file. If the settings at columns 1 and 78 suited all your document needs (which is unlikely), there would be no reason for you to concern yourself with ruler lines.

However, if you don't want margins at columns 1 and 78, you can change the default ruler line settings. Changes can be either temporary or permanent.

GENERAL PROCEDURES

The first two procedures shown below also appear in Units 3 and 4 respectively. They are shown here again for purposes of completeness and handy reference.

To Set Temporary Left and Right Margins in a Document

Temporary ruler lines are stored only for the length of the typing session. When you quit PC-Write, or print your document, the temporary settings are lost.

- Bring a document to the screen.
- Move the cursor to the top of the document.
- Press F2. PC-Write automatically places the cursor in the overwrite mode.
- Move the cursor to the column where you want the left margin and type a capital L. Use the column indicator on the top line to locate the specific column.
- Move the cursor to where you want the right margin and type a capital R.
- Press F2.
- Start or continue typing.

Here is what happens on the screen:

Pressing F2 in the edit mode brings the ruler line to the screen.

Typing capitals L and R in new columns turns the original capitals L and R in columns one and 78 to lowercase. This action disables them as margin-setters.

Pressing F2 removes the ruler line from the screen. The new margins are now set. The text you now type will reflect the new settings.

Note that ruler lines defined with the F2 key are temporary. They must be redefined after you print the file or exit and then reenter the file.

Table 6-1 shows the settings that may be made in the ruler line.

TABLE 6-1 Ruler Line Settings

OPTION	PLACE THIS CHARACTER IN RULER LINE
Set left margin	Place L in desired column
Set right margin ragged	Place R in desired column
Set right margin justified	Place J in desired column
Set paragraph margin	Place P in desired column
Set tab stops	Place T in columns where you want cursor to stop when you press the <tab> key

To Set Permanent Left and Right Margins in a Document

■ Bring a document to the screen.
■ Move the cursor to the top of the document.
■ Press F2. The ruler line appears along with this ruler line menu:

Esc F1:Help F2.Clear F3:To-file F4.Insert F5.Default F6:From-file Grey -

■ Move the cursor to the column where you want the left margin to be and type a capital L.
■ Move the cursor to the column where you want the right margin to be and type a capital R.
■ Press F4. The ruler line settings and its margins are inserted (embedded) in the document.
■ Press F2.
■ Start or continue typing.

Multiple ruler lines with different margin settings can be permanently inserted anywhere in a document. Remember that a ruler line inserted in a document affects all the material typed below it.

Permanent ruler lines are highlighted in the file so they are easy to see. To search for an embedded ruler line, press F2 to bring up the ruler line menu. Then press <Grey+> to search for the next embedded ruler line or press <Grey-> to search for the prior embedded ruler line.

The edit program recognizes an embedded ruler line because the ruler line starts with an Alt-G font character (see Figure 4-3.) Embedded ruler lines are actually regular text characters and therefore such lines can be editied, copied, moved, or deleted just like any other text. However, do not delete the Alt-G font character since it signifies an embedded ruler line to the edit program.

GUIDED ACTIVITY 1   OBSERVING THE LEFT AND RIGHT DEFAULT MARGINS

1. Create the file **DARWIN.DOC**.

2. Press **F2** to bring the default (normal) ruler line to the screen.

3. Notice the letter L in column 1 and the letter R in column 78.

4. Move the cursor to the number 6 on the ruler line and notice the column indicator at the top line shows column 60.

5. Move the cursor to the number 2 on the ruler line and notice the column indicator shows 20.

6. Press **F2** to remove the default ruler line from the screen. Any typing done now will conform to the margins of the ruler line you have just looked at.

7. This activity is completed. Go to step 1 of Guided Activity 2.

Checkpoint

What happens to an existing capital L when another capital L is typed in a new ruler line column?

GUIDED ACTIVITY 2 CHANGING THE LEFT AND RIGHT MARGINS

1. Press **<Home>**

2. We will now put some text in the file. It is taken from Charles Darwin's *The Origin of Species*. Type this:

> **When on board H.M.S. 'Beagle,' as naturalist, I was much struck**
> **with certain facts in the distribution of the organic beings**
> **inhabiting South America, and in the geological relations of the**
> **present to the past inhabitants of that continent...**

3. Notice that left margin text is in column 1. The right margin text is ragged (ends at different columns), but does not extend beyond column 78.

4. Before typing the next paragraph, we will first change the ruler line margins. Press **F2** and move the cursor to column 1.

5. Press **<->** (the minus key), and notice that the L is overwritten.

6. Move the cursor to column 20 and type **L** to set the ruler line at column 20. Remember that all ruler line settings must be in capital letters.

7. Move the cursor to column 60 and type **R** .

8. Notice that the original R at column 78 has been changed to a lowercase r. Lowercase letters have no effect on the ruler line. The L in column 1 could have been disabled in the same manner by typing a capital L in column 20.

9. We will now enter some more Darwin material. Notice the new margin settings.

10. Press **F2**, then press **<Enter>** three times.

11. Type this:

> **These facts...seemed to throw some light on the origin of species
> --that mystery of mysteries... On my return home, it occurred to
> me, in 1837, that something might perhaps be made out on this
> question by patiently accumulating and reflecting on all sorts
> of facts which could possibly have any bearing on it...**

12. Notice that the paragraph appears between margins 20 and 60. If you leave PC-Write and then return, the margin settings *in the ruler line* would be reset to the default values of 1 and 78. Let's observe that the ruler line changes back to the default settings.

13. Exit PC-Write. Bring **DARWIN.DOC** to the screen and press **F2**.

14. Notice that the margins are set at columns 1 and 78. This proves that the margins you set at columns 20 and 60 are no longer in effect. If you want 20 and 60 again, you must again change the ruler line.

15. Quit PC-Write.

This guided activity is completed.

GUIDED ACTIVITY 3 JUSTIFYING THE RIGHT MARGIN

1. Bring the file **DARWIN.DOC** to the screen. Notice the first two paragraphs in the file have ragged right margins. We will set the ruler line to justify the right margin.

PART 1 JUSTIFYING THE RIGHT MARGIN

1. Press **F2**, move the cursor to column 10, and type **L**.

2. Move the cursor to column 65 and type **J**. Capital J is the setting for justifying text.

3. Press **F2**.

4. Press **<Shift>-F7** to turn on automatic paragraph reformatting (Para+).

5. Hold down <**Ctrl**> and press <**PgDn**> twice.

6. Press <**Home**>.

7. Notice that as you type the following material, the right margin is automatically justified. Type this:

> **My work is now (1859) nearly finished; but as it will take me many more months to complete it, and as my health is far from strong, I have been urged to publish this Abstract. I have more especially been induced to do this, as Mr. Wallace, who is now studying the natural history of the Malay Archipelago, has arrived at almost the same general conclusions that I have on the origin of species.**

The little dots you see between some words are PC-Write's way of keeping the words justified between the left margin and the J in the ruler line.

Note: If automatic reformatting had not been turned on in step 4, the text would not have been automatically justified as you typed. In such cases justification is achieved manually by moving the cursor to the top of the paragraph and pressing key F7. The mode to operate in (automatic or manual justifying) is your choice.

To unjustify the right margin, follow the steps in Part 2.

PART 2 UNJUSTIFYING THE RIGHT MARGIN

1. Press **F2**, change the **J** to an **R**, and press **F2**.

2. Move the cursor to the beginning of the third paragraph.

3. Press **F7**. The paragraph is unjustified. The right margin is ragged.

4. Rejustify the paragraph at column 65.

5. Quit PC-Write.

This guided activity is completed.

To Set Permanent Left and Right Margins in the ED.DEF Edit Control File

Many *edit control files* can be created, with each each carrying a different ruler line. Such files are given unique file name extensions. A file thus created, along with its ruler line, will automatically be associated with a *document* file whose extension is identical.

For example, a ruler line in the ED.LTR edit control file will be associated with all documents you create that end in LTR, such as SALES.LTR. When you bring such a document file to the screen, you do not have to set the margins with F2. Such ED files containing ruler lines need be placed on the working disk only, not the data disk.

In the following procedure, the extension LTR is used for example purposes only. Any file name extension (except EXE, COM, or BAT) may be used.

To create a permanent ruler line in an edit control file, proceed as follows:

- Bring the A> prompt to the screen and insert the PC-Write working disk in drive A.
- Type COPY ED.DEF ED.LTR and press <Enter>.
- Type ED ED.LTR and press <Enter>.
- Press <Esc>.
- Change to the overwrite mode.
- Move the cursor to the column where you want the left margin to be and type a capital L.
- Check your cursor location through <Shift>-F9 and then press <Esc> twice.
- Move the cursor to where you want the right margin to be and type a capital R or J.
- Check your cursor location through <Shift>-F9 and then press <Esc> twice.
- Press F1 then F2.

Here is what happens on the screen:

The copy command makes a duplicate of the default ruler line but with a new extension. Typing ED ED.LTR and pressing <Esc> brings the new file to the screen.

You then set the margins where you want them. Using the overstrike mode makes it easier to edit the line.

Saving and quitting through F1 and F2 saves the file with the new ruler line margin settings.

The next time you establish or use a document file with the extension LTR, the ED.LTR edit control file containing the ruler line will automatically be associated with it. You can create as many different edit control file/ruler line combinations as you wish.

Note: When creating a new edit control file such as ED.LTR, you can also establish tab and paragraph settings. See Table 6-1.

GUIDED ACTIVITY 4 SETTING A PERMANENT RULER LINE IN THE ED.DEF FILE

1. Bring the A> prompt to the screen and insert the PC-Write working disk in drive A.

2. Type **COPY ED.DEF ED.LTR** and press **<Enter>**.

3. Type **ED ED.LTR** and press **<Enter>**.

4. Change to the overwrite mode.

5. Move the cursor to column 20 and type a capital **L**.

6. Press **<Shift>-F9** to check your cursor location and then press **<Esc>** twice.

7. Move the cursor to column 65 and type a capital **R**.

8. Press **<Shift>-F9** to check your cursor location and then press **<Esc>** twice.

9. Press **F1** then **F2** to save the file and quit.

10. Insert your data disk in drive B. Type **ED B:SALES.LTR** and press **F9**.

11. Press F2 and note that the margins are set at 20 and 65. This shows that the ED.LTR edit control file you just established will be associated with any document file whose file name extension ends in LTR.

12. Quit PC-Write.

This guided activity is completed.

Checkpoint

If you performed the foregoing guided activity, you now have an ED.LTR edit control file on your working disk. If you create a file and do not use the extension LTR, which edit control file will PC-Write use?

To Set Paragraph Margins

Paragraph margins (Ref. Unit 1, p.7) are set by inserting a P in the ruler line. A ruler line without a P assumes the L as the paragraph margin.

The P sets the margin for the first paragraph line. Subsequent lines in the paragraph use the L as the margin. If there is more than one capital P in the ruler line, the one farthest to the right takes control.

To set paragraph margins, proceed as follows:

- Bring a document to the screen.
- Press F2 and move the cursor to the column where you want the paragraph margin set.
- Type P to set the margin for the *first* line in the paragraph. The *remaining* lines in the paragraph will begin in the column where the L is located.
- Press F2.
- Type your text.

To change paragraph margins in existing text, proceed as follows:

- Press F2.
- Change the P on the ruler line to a Q.
- Type P in the new column.
- Press F2.
- Move the cursor to the beginning of a paragraph and press F7. The first line in the paragraph shifts from the old (Q) position to the new (P) position.

Note: A paragraph setting can also be placed in the ruler line in an edit control file.

GUIDED ACTIVITY 5   SETTING PARAGRAPH MARGINS

1. Create the file **MESSAGE.DOC**.

PART 1 SETTING PARAGRAPH MARGINS

1. Press **F2** and move the cursor to column 10.

2. Type **P** to set the *first* paragraph line at column 10. The *remaining* paragraph lines will begin at column 1, where the L is located.

3. Press **F2**.

4. We will now put text in the file. It is taken from *Sacred Writings*, translated from the Anguttara-Nikaya (iii 35), and is called "Death's Messengers."

Type the text as shown. A double space between lines means a new paragraph. Although the paragraphs are not indented in what follows, they will be when you type them into your file. At the end of each paragraph, press the <Enter> key twice to start a new paragraph.

5. Press <**Shift**>-<**F7**> to turn on automatic paragraph formatting (Para+).

6. Type this:

> **Death has three messengers, O priests. And what are the three?**
>
> **Suppose, O priests, one does evil with his body, does evil with his voice, does evil with his mind...he arrives...after death, at a place of punishment, a place of suffering, perdition, hell. Then, O priests, the guardians of hell seize him...and show him to Yama, the ruler of the dead, saying,**
>
> **"Sire, this man did not do his duty to his friends, to his parents, to the monks, or to the Brahmans, nor did he honor his elders   among his kinfolk.   Let your majesty inflict punishment upon him."**
>
> **Then, O priests, king Yama questions, sounds, and addresses him touching the first of death's messengers.**
>
> **"O man! Did you not see the first of death's messengers visibly appear among men?"**

Notice that each paragraph you have typed is indented at column 10.

Suppose you wanted to change the paragraph indentation from column 10 to column 5. Proceed as follows:

PART 2 CHANGING PARAGRAPH MARGINS

1. Press **F2**.

2. Change the P on the ruler line to a **Q**.

3. Type **P** in column 5.

4. Press **F2**.

5. Move the cursor to the beginning of paragraph one and press **F7**. Observe that the paragraph margin has changed. When a paragraph margin is being changed, the first line in the paragraph shifts from the old (Q) position to the new (P) position.

6. Move the cursor to the beginning of paragraph two and press **F7**. Observe that the paragraph margin has changed.

7. Change the margins in paragraphs three , four, and five.

8. Quit PC-Write.

This guided activity is completed.

To Set Tab Stops

A **tab stop** is a position on the ruler line to which the cursor will move when the <Tab> key is pressed. You place stops by typing a capital T in the ruler line. More than one tab stop can be placed in a ruler line. Tab stops can be erased and repositioned. The default ruler line has stops placed every eight columns starting at column 1, for a total of nine tab stops.

- Bring a document to the screen.
- Press F2.
- Overwrite with a dash the tab stops you do not want.
- Type Ts where you want tab stops.
- Press F2.

Note: Tab stops can also be placed in the ruler line in an edit control file.

GUIDED ACTIVITY 6   SETTING TAB STOPS

1. Bring the **BF.DOC** file to the screen.

2. Notice that the cursor is on the left, in column 1.

3. Press <**Tab**> once; notice that the cursor has jumped to the right.

4. Press <**Tab**> twice; notice that the cursor has jumped twice to the right.

5. Press **F2** and notice the Ts on the ruler line. Every T in the ruler line represents a tab stop location.

6. Let's change the ruler line to four stops every 20 columns, starting in column 1.

7. Press <**Tab**> and then press <**-**> (the minus sign) to overwrite the first T.

8. In a similar manner, overwrite all the remaining Ts.

9. Press **<Home>**, move the cursor to column 20 (use the column indicator as a reference), and type **T**.

10. Place Ts in columns 40, 60, and 80.

11. Press **<Home>**, then **<Tab>** to verify that the cursor stops at positions 20, 40, 60, and 80.

12. Press F2 to remove the ruler line from the screen.

13. Press **<Home>**, then **<Tab>** to verify that the cursor stops at positions 20, 40, 60, and 80.

14. Quit without saving by pressing **F1**, then **F9**, then **F2**.

This guided activity is completed

To Insert Date and Time Automatically

Unit 4 discussed how to insert the current date in your document by using <Alt>-F4 and F5. Here is another way.

- Bring the A> prompt to the screen.
- Insert the PC-Write Working disk in drive A.
- Bring the ED.DEF or similar edit control file to the screen.
- Move to the left margin of the next available line.
- Type the following operation code sequences one below the other. Observe the capitalization. There are no spaces in either line.

    T:566,'HO:MI'
    D:566,'Month D, Year'

- Press F1, then F3 to save the file.
- To verify that the operation codes are correct,

    Move a few lines down the screen.
    Press <Ctrl>-D to insert the current date at the cursor.
    Press <Ctrl>-T to insert the current time at the cursor.

- Delete the current time and date from the screen.
- Quit PC-Write.

The next time you are editing a document, insert the time or date by pressing the appropriate keys.

To Be Reminded Automatically to Save Your Document

- Bring the A> prompt to the screen and insert the PC-Write Working disk in drive A.
- Bring the ED.DEF or similar ruler line to the screen.
- Move to the left margin of the next available line.
- Type the following operation code sequence. Observe the capitalization. There are no spaces in the line.

&M:10

The 10 represents 10 minutes. You can type another number to be reminded at a different time interval.

- Save the ED.DEF or similar file

The next time you are editing a document, you will be reminded every ten minutes to save the file.

Figure 6-2 shows the ED.DEF file with the time, date, and save operation codes entered below the ruler line.

GUIDED ACTIVITY 7   INSERTING DATE, TIME, AND SAVE FUNCTIONS IN AN EDIT CO

Complete Guided Activity 6 before doing this guided activity.

1. Insert the PC-Write working disk in drive A and bring the A> prompt to the screen.

2. Type **ED ED.LTR** to bring the ED.LTR ruler line file to the screen.

3. Insert the date, time, and save operation code sequences, as shown in Figure 6-2.

4. Quit PC-Write.

5. Bring the file **SALES.LTR** to the screen.

6. Press **<Ctrl>-T** to show that the current time appears at the current cursor position.

7. Press **<Ctrl>-D** to show that the current date appears at the current cursor position.

8. Although not necessary to do so, if you were to wait ten minutes, PC-Write would remind you to save the file. Quit PC-Write.

This guided activity is completed.

```
L---+---T1----+-T--2-/\/\/\/\-T5----+-T--6----T----7--T-+--R
T:566,'HO:MI'
D:566,'Month D, Year'
&M:10
```

FIGURE 6-2   THE ED.DEF EDIT CONTROL FILE SHOWING TIME, DATE, AND SAVE OPERATION CODES

HEADERS, FOOTERS, PAGE NUMBERS, AND FOOTNOTES

A header broadly describes a page's contents. A header is printed along the top of the page. A footer also broadly describes a page's contents. A footer is printed at the bottom of the page. A page number is a special header or footer which numerically identifies a page's position in a sequence of pages. A footnote is a note printed at the bottom of a page that comments on the text. A footnote is printed below the text of a page and above a footer. Headers, footers, page numbers, and footnotes all require the use of dot line commands (Ref. Unit 5, p.78).

GENERAL PROCEDURES

To Create a Header

- Bring a document to the screen.
- Move the cursor to column one, or the left margin, at the top of the document. If the first line is occupied by text, insert a blank line above the text.
- Enter a guide line font character by holding down <Alt> and pressing the letter G.
- Type a period, the letter H, a colon, and the header text.

A header dot line placed at the beginning of the document will cause that header to be printed at the top of every page in the document. A header dot line placed elsewhere in the document will affect subsequent pages. Although header lines usually occupy one line, they can occupy two or more lines.

Here is a summary of header dot line commands. Remember that all dot lines must start with the guide line font character.

Dot Line Command	Result
.H:<text>	produces a header line for all pages
.HL:<text>	produces a header line for left-hand pages
.HR:<text>	produces a header line for right-hand pages
.H:	Inserts a blank line at the top of the page
.HQ	Resets to no header lines (turns off header lines)

To Create a footer

- Bring a document to the screen.
- Move the cursor to column one, or the left margin, at the top of the document. If the first line is occupied by text, insert a blank line above the text.
- Enter a guide line font character by holding down <Alt> and pressing the letter G. Type a period, the letter F, a colon, and the footer text.

A footer dot line placed at the beginning of the document will cause that footer to be printed at the bottom of every page in the document. A footer dot line placed elsewhere in the document will affect subsequent pages. Although footer lines usually occupy one line, they can occupy two or more lines.

Here is a summary of footer dot line commands. Remember that all dot lines must start with the guide line font character.

Dot Line Command	Result
.F:<text>	produces a footer line for all pages
.FL:<text>	produces a footer line for left-hand pages
.FR:<text>	produces a footer line for right-hand pages
.F:	Inserts a blank line at the bottom of the page

.FQ   Resets to no footer lines (turns off footer
                                                       lines)

To Print Page Numbers

Page numbers can be printed so they stand alone or as part of a header or footer which contain text. For example, look at the page number location on the first page in this chapter, and then look at the page number location at the top of this page.

Any of the following dot lines will print page numbers. Remember that all dot lines must start with the guide line font character.

Dot Line Command	Result
.HR:$$$	prints a page number at the top, on the right side, of a right-hand page
.HL:$$$	prints a page number at the top, on the left side, of a left-hand page
.H:...$$$...	centers a page number at the top of a page
.FR:$$$	prints a page number at the bottom, on the right side, of a right-hand page
.FL:$$$	prints a page number at the bottom, on the left side, of a left-hand page
.F:...$$$...	centers a page number at the bottom of a page

If any of the above dot lines contained header or footer text, the dollar signs would be placed on the same line. Here is an example which includes the use of an .N dot line to start numbering the pages at 17.

```
.HR:Unit 6  Text and Page Formatting  $$$
.N:17
```

If the .N dot line were left out of the above example, the first page would automatically be numbered 1.

To Create a Footnote

- Bring a document to the screen. Place a footnote reference symbol (e.g <1> or (1)) next to the text on which you wish to comment.
- Type the footnote in a separate paragraph immediately after the paragraph containing the footnote reference symbol. Place a .DB dot line above the footnote paragraph.
- Place a .DQ dot line immediatley below the footnote paragraph.

When the document is printed, the footnote text between the .DB and .DQ dot lines will be moved to the bottom of the page.

Figure 6-3 illustrates a screen configured to create footnotes. Figure 6-4 shows the printed page that results from Figure 6-3.

It is common practice to use a footnote separator to separate footnote text from regular text. A footnote separator is a short horizontal line which starts at the left margin and extends for about one inch. Footnote separators can be placed by using this dot line command: .DH:----------

Place the footnote separator command immediately above the first .DB dot line. Figure 6-5 contains an example of a footnote separator.

The Remote Rescue of Astronauts
Bound for the Moon

There is a little-known story concerning the rescue of
the Apollo XIII Command Module crew through use of the
Lunar Module's electrical power system (1). During the
mission to the moon, an explosion in one of its fuel
tanks knocked out the Command Module's electrical power
system. While the Command module still had the use of
its reentry batteries, they were not nearly large enough
to sustain a return trip to earth. Unless the Lunar
Modules's power system could somehow be tapped, the
astronauts were doomed (2).

.DB
1. The Luner Module used six, large, silver-zinc
   batteries for its electrical power supply. The
   Command Module was fitted with fuel cells for its
   electrical power supply. It also had three small
   batteries for use during earth reentry.

.DQ
.DB
2. Since both spaceships used 28 volt direct current
   electricity, it was indeed possible for one ship to
   use the other's power supply.

.DQ
Fortunately for the crew, and perhaps the entire space
program, a young Grumman Corporation engineer had
foreseen (in 1963) the possibility of having to use the
Lunar Module's power system in just such an emergency
situation (3). When the electrical wiring interface
between the Lunar Module and the Command Module was
being designed, he insisted that the wires be sized not
just to carry operational signals between the two ships,
but to carry the minimum amount of electrical power
necessary to operate the Command Module should it lose
its own power supply. He prevailed, and so did the
astronauts.
.DB
3. The engineer's initials were VPM.

.DQ

FIGURE 6-3 A SCREEN CONTAINING FOOTNOTE COMMANDS

The Remote Rescue of Astronauts
Bound for the Moon

There is a little-known story concerning the rescue of
the Apollo XIII Command Module crew through use of the
Lunar Module's electrical power system (1). During the
mission to the moon, an explosion in one of its fuel
tanks knocked out the Command Module's electrical power
system. While the Command module still had the use of
its reentry batteries, they were not nearly large enough
to sustain a return trip to earth. Unless the Lunar
Modules's power system could somehow be tapped, the
astronauts were doomed (2).

Fortunately for the crew, and perhaps the entire space
program, a young Grumman Corporation engineer had
foreseen (in 1963) the possibility of having to use the
Lunar Module's power system in just such an emergency
situation (3). When the electrical wiring interface
between the Lunar Module and the Command Module was
being designed, he insisted that the wires be sized not
just to carry operational signals between the two ships,
but to carry the minimum amount of electrical power
necessary to operate the Command Module should it lose
its own power supply. He prevailed, and so did the
astronauts.

1. The Luner Module used six, large, silver-zinc
   batteries for its electrical power supply. The
   Command Module was fitted with fuel cells for its
   electrical power supply. It also had three small
   batteries for use during earth reentry.

2. Since both spaceships used 28 volt direct current
   electricity, it was indeed possible for one ship to
   use the other's power supply.

3. The engineer's initials were VPM.

FIGURE 6-4 THE PRINTED PAGE RESULTING FROM THE FOOTNOTE
COMMANDS SHOWN IN FIGURE 6-3

GUIDED ACTIVITY 8   PRINTING PAGE NUMBERS, AND CREATING HEADERS AND FOOTNOTES

1. Create the document file **APOLLO.DOC**.

2. Move to the top of the document and embed a permanent ruler line with margins set at columns 15 (L) and 70 (R).

3. Enter all of material shown in Figure 6-3. Be sure to observe the line spacing within the dot lines, and between the dot lines and the document text. Type your name and the current date at the top of the page above the title.

4. Move to the first line below the embedded ruler line and enter the following dot line commands. Be sure to precede each dot line with the guide line font character by holding down <Alt> and pressing the letter G.

   .F:...$$$...   (will print a centered page number)
   .HR: (will leave a space above the header)
   .HR:The Apollo Moon Landing Program   (will print a header)
   .HR: (will leave a space after the header)

5. Print the document. Verify the following:

   a) Your name and the current date are at the top of the page.
   b) Three footnotes are at the bottom of the page.
   c) A page number is present at the bottom of the page.
   d) A header is present at the top of the page.

6. Quit PC-Write.

Application

In this application you will use the BALANCE.DOC file created in Unit 4, Guided Activity 3. You will add headers, page numbers, and footnotes to BALANCE.DOC. When you complete this application assignment, your printed document should look like the one shown in Figure 6-5.

PART 1 ADDING HEADERS AND PAGE NUMBERS

BALANCE.DOC is two pages long. On the first (right-hand) page add the header "The Balance Sheet." On the second (left-hand) page add the header "Financial Statements." Add centered page numbers at the bottom of the page.

Design the header locations so that they start printing two spaces from the top of the page. This will require the use of two blank header lines for each page (i.e two ".HR:"s and two ".HL:"s). To provide space between the header and the text at the top of the second page, use two additional blank .HL: lines. For consistency, add two equivalent lines to the right-hand (first) page as well. These blank header lines must be properly placed to achieve the effect shown in Figure 6-5..

Print the document. Don't be afraid to make a mistake. Try something, print it, and revise it as necessary. Complete Part 1 before trying Part 2.

PART 2 ADDING FOOTNOTES

Place a footnote symbol next to the word "owners" in the next-to-last line in paragraph two. The associated footnote should read "A company can have one owner (a sole proprietorship), several owners (a partnership), or many owners (a corporation)."

Place another footnote symbol next to "retained earnings" near the end of the document. The associated footnote should read "Retained earnings are those earnings not paid to owners. They are retained by the company for use by the company."

Use a footnote separator. Insert page breaks. Print the document. Use Figure 6-5 to check your answer .

The Balance Sheet

A DESCRIPTION OF A
BALANCE SHEET

Prepared by: (type your name here)
  (insert the current date here)

A balance sheet shows the result of operating a
company over a given period of time. The time
period is usually one year.   A balance sheet has
three parts: assets, liabilities, and capital.

Assets are valuable things owned by the company.
Liabilities are debts owed by the company to
banks and claims against it by suppliers
(trade creditors).   Capital is the amount of
the company's assets (after paying all
liabilities) that would be divided among
owners if the company were sold or went out of
business.

The balance sheet is important because it shows how
well a company is operating. It shows the
proportion of all the company's assets owned by or
owed to its trade creditors, banks, and owners. If
the proportion owned by owners <1> increases, the
company is doing well.

Examples of assets are:

 - Bank accounts

 - Accounts payable (amounts due from customers)

 - Inventories

 - Property, plant, and equipment

 - Copyrights and patents

----
1. A company can have one owner (a sole
   proprietorship), several owners (a partnership),
   or many owners (a corporation).
      1

**FIGURE 6-5 THE SOLUTION (Page 1 only), TO APPLICATION D SHOWING A
HEADER, A PAGE NUMBER, AND A FOOTNOTE**

REVIEW QUESTIONS

1. What is an edit control file?

   _____

   _____

2. What is the file name of the edit control file that is automaticaaly placed on the working disk?

   _____

3. In which ruler line columns do the default margins appear?

   _____

4. What is the procedure for placing a customized permanent ruler line in an edit control file?

   _____

   _____

   _____

   _____

5. What do the characters **&M:20** represent?

   _____

   _____

6. What does a capital J in a ruler line signify?

   _____

7. Describe the procedure for setting a paragraph margin.

   _____

   _____

8. What is a tab stop?

_____

_____

9. How are Tab stops established?

_____

_____

10. Describe the following document features.

  a. Header

  _____

  _____

  b. Footer

  _____

  _____

  c. Footnote

  _____

  _____

11. What function is served by this dot line command? .DH:----------

_____

_____

12. If you had two or more footnotes on the same page, how would you provide a space between each footnote? (Hint: look at Figure 6-3.)

_____

_____

DOCUMENTATION RESEARCH

Consult the PC-Write manual on each of the following items and record the answer in the space provided.

1. How can temporary left and right margins be set without using the ruler line?

_____

_____

2. Table 6-1 shows certain settings that can be made in a ruler line. Identify other settings that can be made.

_____

_____

_____

_____

_____

_____

_____

_____

_____

3. How can the word "Page" be made to appear next to a page number?

_____

_____

4. What happens when there is not enough space on the bottom of a page to print a foot-note?

_____

---

5. Footnotes are normally printed with a single space between lines. How can they be made to print with two or more spaces between lines.?

UNIT 7

COPYING AND MOVING TEXT

LEARNING OBJECTIVES

Upon completion of this unit you should know how to

1. copy text within a document.

2. copy text from one document to another document.

3. create a new file with marked text.

4. move text within a document.

UNIT OUTLINE

Learning Objectives

Unit Outline

Introduction

General Procedures

    Copying Text

        To Copy Text Within a Document

        To Copy Text From One Document to Another Document

        To Create a New File With Marked Text

    Moving Text

        To Move Text Within a Document

Application E

Review Questions

Documentation Research

INTRODUCTION

Copying text means reproducing text in another place. The copied text remains in its original position as well as in its new position. **Moving** text means relocating text from one place to another. The text moved is no longer in its original location.

GENERAL PROCEDURES

COPYING TEXT

To Copy Text Within a Document

- Bring the document to the screen.
- Move the cursor to the beginning of the text to be copied and press F3.
- Move the cursor to the end of the text to be copied and press F3.
- Move the cursor to where you want the text to appear and Press F3.
- Press F5

Here is what happens on the screen.

Moving the cursor to the beginning of the text and pressing F3 starts the marking process. The top line reads "MARKING."

Moving the cursor to the end of the text to be copied causes the text to be highlighted. Pressing F3 stops the marking process. The top line reads "MARKED." The marked text must be contiguous. For example, in a series of three paragraphs, these may be marked:

1, 2, and 3   OR   1 and 2   OR   2 and 3.

Paragraphs 1 and 3 may not be marked.

Only one block of text may be marked at a time.

Moving the cursor to a new location and pressing F3 causes the marked text to appear at that location. While the text is marked, the cursor can be moved to another location, and the same text can be copied there. Pressing F5 unmarks the text and completes the copy operation.

GUIDED ACTIVITY 1   COPYING TEXT WITHIN A DOCUMENT

In this activity we will create a document (taken from Christopher Columbus's letter regarding his discovery, sent to the treasurer of Spain) and then practice copying text.

Figure 7-1 shows the result of this guided activity.

1. Create the file **COLUMBUS.DOC**, and embed a permanent ruler line with margins at 15 (L) and 65 (R). The paragraphs in your document will be slightly narrower than those shown below in boldface.

2. Type this:

> **THE LETTER OF COLUMBUS**
> **To Luis De Sant Angel**
> **Announcing His Discovery**
> **(1493)**

> **Sir: As I know you will be rejoiced at the glorious**
> **success that our Lord has given me in my voyage, I write this**
> **to tell you how in thirty-three days I sailed to the Indies**
> **with the fleet that the illustrious King and Queen, our**
> **Sovereigns, gave me,   where I discovered a great many**
> **islands, inhabited by numberless   people; and of all I**
> **have taken possession for their Highnesses   by proclamation**
> **and display of the Royal Standard without opposition.**

> **To the first island I discovered I gave the name of San**
> **Salvador, in commemoration of His Divine Majesty, who has**
> **wonderfully granted all this.   The indians call it Guanaham.**
> **The second I named the Island of Santa Maria de Conceptcion;**
> **the third, Fernandina; the fourth, Isabella; the fifth,**
> **Juana...**

> **...When I came to Juana, I followed the coast of that isle**
> **toward the west...I continued the said route (and found) that**
> **the coast led northward...**

3. Save the document.

4. Verify that the cursor is at the end of the last line and press **<Enter>** three times.

5. Type **Names of Islands Mentioned in Above Passage**

6. Move the cursor to the "N" in "Names", hold down <Alt>, and press the letter B.

7. Repeat step 6 at the space following the "e" in "Passage." The material you typed in step 5 will appear in boldface (dark print) when printed.

8. Move the cursor to the "S" in "San", press **F3**, then press **<Down Arrow>**.

9. Press **<Left Arrow>** until the cursor is just to the right of the "r" in "Salvador", then press **F3**. San Salvador is now marked.

10. Position the cursor two lines below the "N" in "Names" and press **F3**. Place the cursor on the "n" in "San", press **<Right Arrow>** twice, and then press **<Del>**.

11. Press **F5**.

12. Copy all the remaining island names, including Guanaham, listing one below the other.

13. Verify that the cursor is next to the "a" in "Juana" at the end of the list, and press **<Enter>** three times.

14. Type **Island names compiled by (your name and date)**.

15. Print the document and quit PC-Write.

This guided activity is completed.

Checkpoint

As long as marked text remains marked, it can be copied over and over again to different locations (true or false?).

To Copy Text From One Document to Another Document

Use this procedure to copy text from one file to another <u>existing</u> file.

■ Bring a document to the screen.
■ Move the cursor to the beginning of the text to be copied and press F3.
■ Move the cursor to the end of the text to be copied and press F3.
■ Press F1.
■ Press F6.
■ Type the name of the receiving file and press <Enter>.
■ Press <Esc>.
■ Move the cursor to desired location in the receiving file.
■ Press <Ctrl> and F4.
■ Press F5.

THE LETTER OF COLUMBUS
To Luis De Sant Angel
Announcing His Discovery
(1493)

Sir: As I know you will be rejoiced at the
glorious success that our Lord has given me in my
voyage, I write this to tell you how in thirty-
three days I sailed to the indies with the fleet
that the illustrious King and Queen, our
Sovereigns, gave me,   where I discovered a great
many islands,   inhabited by numberless people;
and of all I have taken possession for their
Highnesses by proclamation and display of the
Royal Standard without opposition.

To the first island I discovered I gave the
name of San Salvador, in commemoration of His
Divine Majesty, who has wonderfully granted all
this. The indians call it Guanaham. The second
I named the Island of Santa Maria de Conceptcion;
the third, Fernandina; the fourth, Isabella;
the fifth, Juana...

...When I came to Juana, I followed the coast of
that isle toward the west...I continued the said
route (and found) that the coast led northward...

Names of Islands Mentioned in Above Passage

San Salvador
(Guanaham)

Santa Maria de Conceptcion

Fernandina

Isabella

Juana

Island names compiled by (Name), (Date)

FIGURE 7-1 COLUMBUS.DOC, THE RESULT OF GUIDED ACTIVITY 1

GUIDED ACTIVITY 2 COPYING TEXT FROM ONE DOCUMENT TO ANOTHER

In this guided activity, the names of people appearing on one document will be copied to another document. The files for this activity are already on your data disk.

Figure 7-2 shows the result of this guided activity.

1. Bring the file **DECLARA.DOC** to the screen.

2. Note that an excerpt from the <u>Declaration of Independence</u> is on the screen. We will copy the names of those who signed the declaration to another document, titled Signers of American Historical Documents.

3. Move the cursor to the "J" in "John Hancock" (near the top of the document's second page) and press F3 to begin marking text.

4. Press **<Down Arrow>** until all names are highlighted. Then press **F3** to complete marking text.

5. Press **F1**, then **F6**.

6. Notice that you are asked for a file name to load or create. In this instance, we want to load SIGNERS.DOC, an existing document that will receive the marked names.

7. Type **B:SIGNERS.DOC**. Press **<Enter>**, and then press **<Esc>**. You are now in the receiving document.

8. Move the cursor to the end of the heading "Signers of the Declaration of Independence" and press **<Enter>** twice.

9. Press **<Ctrl>** and **F4**. The names appear in the document. They are still in the original sending document, as well.

10. Press **F5** to unmark the text. Align John Hancock's name with the left margin.

11. Move the cursor to the end of the last document line and press **<Enter>** three times.

12. Type and make bold **List compiled by (your name and date)**.

13. Insert page breaks, save, and print the document.

This guided activity is completed.

Checkpoint

Which document is brought to the screen first, the document that will "send" the text, or the document that will "receive" the text.

The Signers of American Historical Documents

Signers of the Declaration of Independence

John Hancock

New Hampshire
Josiah Bartlett   Matthew Thorton
Wm. Whipple

Massachusetts Bay
Saml. Adams   Elbridge Gerry
John Adams   Robt. Treat Paine

Rhode Island
Step. Hopkins   William Ellery

Connecticut
Roger Sherman   Wm. Williams
Sam'el Huntington   Oliver Wolcott

New York
Wm. Floyd   Frans. Lewis Phil.
Livingston   Lewis Morris

New Jersey
Richd. Stockton   John Hart
Jno. Witherspoon   Abra. Clark
Fras. Hopkinson

Pennsylvania
Robt. Morris   Jas. Smith
Benjamin Rush   Geo. Taylor
Benja. Franklin   James Wilson
John Morton   Geo. Ross
Geo. Clymer

Delaware
Caesar Rodney   Tho. M'Kean
Geo. Read

Maryland
Samuel Chase   Thos. Stone
Wm. Paca

FIGURE 7-2 SIGNERS.DOC (Page 1 only), THE RESULT OF GUIDED ACTIVITY 2

To Create a New File With Marked Text

To create a <u>new</u> file with marked text, use this procedure:

- Bring a document to the screen.
- Move the cursor to the beginning of the text to be marked and press <Ctrl>-F6.

- Move cursor to end of text to be marked and press <Ctrl>-<F6>.

The top line reads

      Copy mark text to file (Esc: cancel F8:dir): "mark.doc"

- Use mark.doc as the new file name--or type a new one--and press <Enter>. Precede the file name by the disk drive letter and a colon.
- Press F5 to unmark the text.

    The edit status line returns to the top of the screen and the original file remains on the screen. To edit the newly created file do this:

- Leave the current file.
- Bring the new file to the screen and edit as appropriate.

GUIDED ACTIVITY 3 CREATING A NEW FILE WITH MARKED TEXT

In this guided activity the names of people appearing on one document will be marked and then used to create another, new, document. The sending file for this activity is already on your data disk. You will create the receiving file as part of the activity.

1. Bring the file **DECLARA.DOC** to the screen.

2. Note that an excerpt from the <u>Declaration of Independence</u> is on the screen. We will copy the names of those who signed the declaration to another document which does not now exist, but which you will create.

3. Move the cursor to the "J" in "John Hancock" (near the top of the document's second page), and press **<Ctrl>** and **<F6>**. This marks the beginning of the text. Notice that the top line says "Marking."

4. Press **<Down Arrow>** until all names are highlighted; then, press **<Ctrl>** and **F6**. Marking of text is completed.

5. Type **B:SIGN.DOC** and press **<Enter>**. The new document is created containing the marked names.

6. Press **F5** to unmark the text.

7. Press **F1**, then **F6** to prepare to load SIGN.DOC.

8. Type **B:SIGN.DOC**, press **<Enter>**, and then press **<Esc>**.

9. Set the margins at 15 (L) and 65 (R). Remove the page marker to the left of "Maryland."

10. Use Figure 7-3 as a guide and edit the document as follows:

    Add a title line at line 1 and a name and date line at line 2.

    Delete a blank line between each set of names and the name of a state.

Rearrange the text so that it lines up at column 15. Only one name requires retyping (Wm. Whipple). Arrange all other names using <space bar> in pushright mode and <Delete>.

The edited document should look like Figure 7-3.

11. Print the document and quit PC-Write.

This guided Activity is completed.

Checkpoint

What message does PC-Write provide after <Ctrl>-F6 is pressed a second time?

_____

MOVING TEXT

While text can be copied from one file (document) to another, it can be moved only within the same document. The procedure described below is similar to the copy procedure, except that key F6 is used instead of key F3.

To Move Text Within a Document

■ Bring the document to the screen.
■ Move the cursor to the beginning of the text to be moved and press F6.
■ Move the cursor to the end of the text to be moved and press F6.
■ Move the cursor to the text's new location and press F6.
■ Press F5.

A New File of Famous Signers
Prepared by (Name), (Date)

John Hancock

New Hampshire
Josiah Bartlett   Matthew Thorton
Wm. Whipple

Massachusetts Bay
Saml. Adams   Elbridge Gerry
John Adams   Robt. Treat Paine

Rhode Island
Step. Hopkins   William Ellery

Connecticut
Roger Sherman   Wm. Williams
Sam'el Huntington   Oliver Wolcott

New York
Wm. Floyd   Frans. Lewis Phil.
Livingston   Lewis Morris

New Jersey
Richd. Stockton   John Hart
Jno. Witherspoon   Abra. Clark
Fras. Hopkinson

Pennsylvania
Robt. Morris   Jas. Smith
Benjamin Rush   Geo. Taylor
Benja. Franklin   James Wilson
John Morton   Geo. Ross
Geo. Clymer

Delaware
Caesar Rodney   Tho. M'Kean
Geo. Read

Maryland
Samuel Chase   Thos. Stone
Wm. Paca

Virginia
George Wythe   Thos. Nelson, jr.
Richard Henry Lee   Francis Lightfoot Lee
Th. Jefferson   Carter Braxton
Benja. Harrison

North Carolina
Wm. Hooper   John Penn
Joseph Hewes

South Carolina
Edward Rutledge   Arthur Middleton
Thos. Heyward, junr Thomas Lynch, junr

Georgia
Burton Gwinnett   Geo. Walton
Lyman Hall

FIGURE 7-3 SIGN.DOC, THE RESULT OF GUIDED ACTIVITY 3

GUIDED ACTIVITY 4 MOVING TEXT WITHIN A DOCUMENT

1. Load the file **NOTRIGHT.DOC**.

2. Embed a permanent ruler line with margins at 10 (L) and 78 (R).

3. Notice that the amendments to the Constitution are not listed in proper numerical order.

4. Move the amendments and put them in proper numerical order.

5. Rename the file **RIGHTS.DOC**.

6. Save and print the file.

7. Quit PC-Write.

This guided activity is completed.

Checkpoint

Text to be moved can be marked using F3 and then moved using F6. Explain why.

_____

_____

Application

Locate copies of any two of the following documents. If necessary, ask your community or college librarian for help.

Articles of Confederation

Articles of Capitulation Yorktown

Treaty of Great Britain

Constitution of the United States

Copy the names of those who signed the documents onto a piece of paper. Copy the names in two columns, one for each document. Label each column with the name of its associated document.

Create a separate file for each column. Copy each file into the SIGNERS.DOC file under its proper heading. Rename SIGNERS.DOC to SIGNERSX.DOC. Change the last line in the document to read:

Expanded list compiled by (your name and date)

Insert page breaks in SIGNERSX.DOC, save, and print the document.

REVIEW QUESTIONS

1. What is the difference between copying text and moving text?

_____

_____

2. What is meant by the statement "marked text must be contiguous"?

_____

_____

3. How many different blocks of text may be marked at the same time?

_____

4. What two keys can be used to start and stop marking text?

_____

5. What key is used to copy marked text?

_____

6. What key is used to move marked text?

_____

7. What key is used to unmark text?

_____

8. The screen gives <u>two</u> clues to show that text has been marked. What are they?

_____

_____

9. Can text be moved from one document to another?

_____

10. What is the procedure for copying text from one part of a document to another part of the same document?

_____

_____

_____

11. What is the procedure for copying text from one document to another, existing, document.

_____

_____

_____

_____

_____

_____

_____

_____

12. What is the procedure for creating a new document with marked text?

_____

_____

_____

_____

DOCUMENTATION RESEARCH

A hold area is a portion of computer memory that can store text temporarily. Consult the PC-Write manual for the discussion on moving a block of text by using F4 and the hold area. Summarize the procedure here.

_____

_____

_____

Consult the PC-Write manual for the discussion on how to print marked text. Summarize the procedure here.

_____

_____

_____

UNIT

8

FINDING AND REPLACING TEXT

LEARNING OBJECTIVES

Upon completion of this unit you should know how to

1. change text through the Find and Replace function.

2. restore replaced text.

3. find text without changing.

4. display the current cursor position.

5. move the cursor to a new location.

6. set a bookmark.

UNIT OUTLINE

INTRODUCTION

Text can be changed with the Find and Replace function in one of three ways: a) Find text and automatically change all occurrences, b) find text and automatically change it one occurrence at a time, or c) find text and then decide whether or not to change it.

Text can also be restored if it is has been changed mistakenly or if you decide you prefer the original text. Bookmarks can be established with which you can automatically send the cursor to a specified document location. The following provides the general procedures for finding and replacing text, restoring text, and establishing bookmarks.

GENERAL PROCEDURES

FINDING AND REPLACING TEXT

To Find and Automatically Change All Occurrences of Text

- Bring a document to the screen.
- Move the cursor to the beginning of the text to be searched.
- Press <Esc> to bring up the Esc main menu.
- Press F9.
- Type the exact text you want to find.
- Press Fl0.
- Type the replacement (new) text.
- Press <Enter>.

This completes the Find and Replace "set-up." The next step is to actually perform the Find and Replace operation.

- Press <ALT>-Fl0.
- Press F9.
- Press F5.

Here is what happens on the screen:

Moving the cursor to the beginning of the text to be searched ensures that all occurrences of the Find text will be replaced with the Replace text.

Pressing <Esc> brings up the Esc main menu.

Pressing F9 brings up the Find and Replace menu:

     Esc F9:Find"." Fl0:Replace:"."

You now type the Find text inside the quotation marks.

Pressing Fl0 causes the cursor to jump to the Replace portion of the Find and Replace menu. You now type the replacement text inside the Replace quotation marks.

Pressing <Enter> returns the cursor to the document.

This completes the Find and Replace "set-up." The next step is to actually perform the Find and Replace operation.

Pressing <Alt>-Fl0 results in the following:

   If the Find text is not found, the top line will read "Did not find"; otherwise, the top line shows:

     Esc:cancel F9:Repeat-replace Fl0:Un-replace

Pressing F9 causes every occurrence of the Find text to be replaced by the Replace text. (Note: If any text happens to be marked, the top line will show: Esc: Cancel F9: Within-marked Fl0: Everywhere. Press F9 to replace only within the marked text. Press Fl0 to replace every occurrence of the Find text).

As each occurrence is found and replaced, it is quickly shown on the screen. When the Find and Replace operation is completed, the top line shows:

     Find "old" Replace "new"; repeated, X times

Pressing F5 unmarks the last replaced text. You are now back in the edit mode.

FIND AND REPLACE POINTERS

Setting Boundaries Pressing F6 before and after typing the Find text causes a **boundary symbol** (a small square with a circle in its middle) to surround the Find text.

The boundary symbol ensures that you will find and replace only the text you want, and not text which appears similar. For example, if you want to find "old," the boundary symbol ensures that you will not also find "hold", "bold", or "fold." Here is a summary of how text is found and replaced:

If find text is	This text is found
All lower case	Any combination of lower- and uppercase
All upper case	All uppercase

Mixed case	Uppercase finds uppercase, lowercase finds lowercase

If found text is	PC-Write Replaces as
All lowercase	All lowercase
All uppercase	All uppercase
Mixed case	First letter matched to Find text; all others follow Replace text

Here are some Find and Replace examples:

Find text	Replace text	Text in document	Replaced as
old	mature	old	mature
OLD	mature	OLD	MATURE
Old	mature	Old	Mature

Reformatting Automatic reformatting is not active when you are finding and replacing every occurrence. It may therefore be necessary to reformat all paragraphs if the lengths of the Find and Replace texts are too unequal. If necessary, reformat all paragraphs by first pressing <Ctrl>-F5, then F7, then F5 (Caution: this procedure automatically reformats the entire document--see Item 1 in the Documentation Research section at the end of this Unit). Such reformatting may require repaging via (ALT)-F7.

Restoring Changed Text Suppose you make a mistake when typing the replacement text. For example, instead of typing "mature" as the replacement text, you type "eggroll" and then proceed with the Find and Replace operation. One way to fix the problem is to type "eggroll" as the new Find text and "mature" as the new Replacement text and implement the Find and Replace operation. All occurrences are changed back, and the document is restored.

Another approach is to let PC-Write swap the Find and Replace texts and then perform the Find and Replace operation again:

■ Press Ctrl-Fl0.

The top line shows the original Replace text in the Find in position, and the original Find text in the Replace position.

■ Press <ALT>-Fl0.
■ Press F9.

All occurrences are changed back, and the document is restored.

To "unreplace" *one* piece of text accidentally changed, proceed as follows:

- Place the cursor just after the replaced text.
- Press (ALT)-Fl0.
- Top line shows: ESC:Cancel F9: Repeat-replace Fl0: Un-replace
- Press Fl0 and the text is restored.

Finding and automatically replacing *all* occurrences of the Find text is covered in the foregoing section. Finding and automatically replacing only the *next* occurrence, or finding first, *then* deciding to replace, are covered next.

To Find and Automatically Change One Occurrence of Text

- Bring a document to the screen.
- Press <Esc> to bring up the Esc main menu.
- Press F9.
- Press F6.
- Type the exact text you want to find.
- Press F6.
- Press Fl0.
- Type the replacement (new) text.
- Press <Enter>.

This completes the Find and Replace "set-up." The next step is to actually perform the Find and Replace operation.

- Press <Grey + > to search forward in the document or <Grey -> to search backward.
- Press F10.
- Repeat as desired.

To Find Text and Then Decide to Make a Change

- Bring a document to the screen.
- Press <Esc> to bring up the Esc main menu.
- Press F9.
- Press F6.
- Type the exact text you want to find.
- Press F6.
- Press Fl0.
- Type the replacement (new) text.
- Press <Enter>.

This completes the Find and Replace" set-up." The next step is to actually perform the Find and Replace operation.

- Press < Grey + > to search forward in the document or < Grey -> to search backward.
- When the text is found, press F10 to replace, or
- Press < Grey + > or < Grey -> for next occurrence.

To Find Text Without Changing

Sometimes you may want to find text without replacing. You might have any of the following reasons. You might want to see if a certain word, phrase, or name is used in a document, or to see how a word, phrase, a name is used in context. Or you may just want to go to a certain location in a document in order to edit text. In such cases, proceed as follows:

- Bring a document to the screen.
- Press < Alt >-< White + > to move to the top of the document.
- Press < Esc > to bring up the Esc Main Menu.
- Press F9.
- Press F6.
- Type the exact text you want to find.
- Press F6.
- Press < Enter >. The cursor returns to the document.

This completes the Find "set-up." The next step is to actually perform the Find operation.

- Press < Grey + >.

    If found, the text is highlighted. If not found, the top line reads "did not find 'find' text."

GUIDED ACTIVITY 1 Finding and Automatically Changing All Occurrences
of Text

In the following material, do not type the quotation marks.

1. Create the file **LEAD.DOC**.

2. Embed a permanent ruler line with margins at 20 (L) and 60 (J). Set automatic reformatting of paragraphs on (Para+).

3. Type this:

Facts About Xx

Xx is a metallic element. It is soft, dense, malleable, ductile and blue-white in color. Xx is extracted mainly from galena. It is used in the manufacture of containers and pipes as an anti-corrosive, and in solder, bullets, paints, and radiation shields.

Xx has an atomic number of 82. The atomic weight of xx is 207.l9. Xx melts at 327.5 degrees centigrade and boils at 1,744 degrees centigrade. The specific gravity of xx is ll.35.

4. Your typed document should look like Figure 8-1.

```
      Facts About Xx

Xx is a metallic element.  It is soft,
dense, malleable, ductile and blue-white
in color.  Xx is extracted mainly from
galena.  It is used in the manufacture of
containers and pipes as an anti-
corrosive, and in solder, bullets,
paints, and radiation shields.

Xx has an atomic number of 82.  The
atomic weight of xx is 207.l9.  Xx melts
at 327.5 degrees centigrade and boils at
1,744 degrees centigrade.  The specific
gravity of xx is ll.35.
```

FIGURE 8-1 LEAD.DOC, THE RESULT OF STEP 3, GUIDED ACTIVITY 1

5. Change every occurrence of "Xx" or "xx" to "Lead" or "lead."

   Hint: Use "Xx" as the Find text and "Lead" as the Replace text. Then use "xx" as the Find text and "lead" as the Replace text. Reformat the paragraphs.

6. When step 5 is completed, your document should look like Figure 8-2.

Facts About Lead

Lead is a metallic element. It is soft,
dense, malleable, ductile and blue-white
in color. Lead is extracted mainly from
galena. It is used in the manufacture of
containers and pipes as an anti-
corrosive, and in solder, bullets,
paints, and radiation shields.

Lead has an atomic number of 82. The
atomic weight of lead is 207.19. Lead
melts at 327.5 degrees centigrade and
boils at 1,744 degrees centigrade. The
specific gravity of lead is 11.35.

FIGURE 8-2 LEAD.DOC, THE RESULT OF STEP 5, GUIDED ACTIVITY 1

7. Find the word "extracted."

8. Change the word "extracted" to "obtained."

9. Add your name and the current date at the bottom of the document.

10. Print the document and quit PC-Write.

This guided activity is completed.

Checkpoint

How would you restore "Lead" to "Xx?"

CURSOR ESCAPADES

To Display the Current Cursor Location

■ Bring a document to the screen.

- Move the cursor below any dot lines that may appear at the beginning of the document. This is to ensure that the correct current page number is displayed.
- Press <Shift>-F9.
- Read the cursor location on the top line.
- Press <Esc>.
- Press <Esc>.

See Figure 8-3 for a sample result of pressing <Shift>-F9.

Line 296/358 in file. Column 65/78. Line 41/57 on Page 118/120

FIGURE 8-3 THE TOP LINE SHOWING A SAMPLE CURRENT CURSOR LOCATION

In Figure 8-3, 296/358 means that there are 358 lines in the document file and the cursor is on line 296. The number 358 includes every line from the beginning of the file, including dot lines. There are 78 columns in the current ruler line, and the cursor is in column 65. The current page has 57 lines, and the cursor is on line 41. There are 120 pages in the document, and the cursor is on page 118.

To Jump to a New Line, Column, or Page

- Bring a document to the screen.
- Move the cursor below any dot lines that may appear at the beginning of the document.
- Press <Alt>-F9.
- Press F7 (for new line anywhere in the document), F8 (for new column), F9 (for new line on current page), or F10 (for new page).
- Type the new line, column, or page number.
- Press <Enter> or <Grey + >.

See Figure 8-4 for a sample result of pressing <Alt>-F9.

F7:Line 325/386 in file. F8:Column 10/78. F9:Line 13/57 on F10:Page 119/121

**FIGURE 8-4 THE TOP LINE SHOWING A SAMPLE CURRENT CURSOR LOCATION
           AND JUMP CHOICES**

In Figure 8-4, 325/386 means that there are 386 lines in the document file and the cursor is on line 325. The number 386 includes every line from the beginning of the file, including dot lines. There are 78 columns in the current ruler line, and the cursor is in column 10. The current page has 57 lines, and the cursor is on line 3. There are 121 pages in the document, and the cursor is on page 119.

To Jump Automatically to a New Location (Set a Bookmark)

PC-Write can jump automatically to a predetermined location. A predetermined location is called a bookmark. Once a bookmark is set, you can return automatically to the marked location from anywhere in the document. Bookmarks last only for the current editing session. They are not saved with the file.

- Move the cursor to the place to which you want to jump.
- Press <Ctrl>-<Home>.

  The location is marked.

- Continue typing or move the cursor to a new location.
- Press <Ctrl>-<End> to return to the bookmark.

To set a second bookmark, do the following:

- Move the cursor to the second location.
- Press <Shift>-<Ctrl>-<Home>.

  The second location is marked

- Continue typing or move the cursor to a new location.
- Press <Shift>-<Ctrl>-<End> to return to the second bookmark.

Application

Perform the following Find and Replace, and cursor operations with the file LEAD.DOC on the screen.

1. A temperature of 327.5 degrees centigrade is equivalent to 621.5 degrees fahrenheit. On this basis, change the value "327.5" to 621.5, and change the value "1,744" to 3,171.2. Change all occurrences of "centigrade" to "fahrenheit." Change "color" to "appearance," and "mainly" to "primarily." Save and print the document.

2. Move the cursor to the "s" in "solder" in the first paragraph, and display the current cursor location. Copy the contents of the top line to the line below.

_____

3. Press <Home> and then jump to the fourth line in paragraph two.

4. Jump to column 25.

5. Set a bookmark for the word "malleable" in the first paragraph.

6. Set a second bookmark for the word "gravity" in the the second paragraph.

7. Jump to the first bookmark.

8. Jump to the second bookmark.

REVIEW QUESTIONS

1. Describe three ways to find and replace text.

_____

_____

_____

2. What is the purpose of the F6 boundary symbol?

_____

_____

3. Draw a picture of the F6 boundary symbol here:

_____

4. Under what condition may it be necessary to reformat paragraphs after a Find and Replace operation?

_____

5. List the procedure to find and automatically change all occurrences of text.

_____

_____

_____

_____

_____

_____

_____

6. What is the procedure for setting a bookmark?

_____

_____

DOCUMENTATION RESEARCH

1. Consult the PC-Write manual on how to keep a block of text from reformatting. Record the procedure here.

_____

_____

_____

_____

2. PC-Write calls the boundary symbol represented by function key F6 a "wild card." Actually, PC-Write has more than one boundary symbol or wild card. Each wild card represents a different search condition. Find the topic "Searching with Wild Cards" in the the PC-Write manual. List below the search condition each function key represents.

F2 _____

F3 _____

F4 _____

F5 _____

F6 _____

F7 _____

F8 _____

UNIT
9
ENHANCING TEXT

LEARNING OBJECTIVES

Upon completion of this unit you should know how to

1. use text-embedded commands to

   a) underline

   b) boldface

   c) enlarge

   d) reduce

   e) enclose.

2. use global dot commands to

   a) underline

   b) boldface

   c) enlarge

   d) reduce.

UNIT OUTLINE

Unit Outline

Introduction

Fundamentals of Text Enhancement

General Procedures

    Embedded Commands

        To Underline

        To Draw a line

        To Boldface

        To Enlarge

        To Reduce

        To Enclose

    Global Dot Commands

        To Underline

        To Boldface

        To Enlarge

        To Reduce

Enhancement Pointers

Application G

Review Questions

Documentation Research

INTRODUCTION

Enhancing text means causing selected text to stand out from surrounding text. Enhancements are used to promote understanding in the reader. These are some common reasons for enhancing text:

1. To draw attention

2. To emphasize

3. To promote clarity

4. To improve appearance.

The writer must have a reason for enhancing text in the context of what is being written. For example, to simply underline words in a passage without some overall plan will confuse the reader. Too many enhancements in a given block of text can easily confound a reader. However, underlining topic headings in a report, or boldfacing action items in a business memo, can be effective. Enhancements are helpful to the reader when used sparingly and for the reasons cited above.

FUNDAMENTALS OF TEXT ENHANCEMENT

Text is made to stand out from the text around it through differences in the appearance of its print. Here are some approaches to enhancing text:

1. Underlining

2. Boldfacing (text prints darker than surrounding text)

3. Enlarging

4. reducing

5. Enclosing

PC-Write has two document-based approaches to enhancing text. They are embedded and global. The embedded approach places commands directly in the body of the text and affects only local words. The global approach places dot commands in the left margins of documents. These commands affect larger blocks of text, such as lines, paragraphs, and pages.

Some enhancements do not appear on the screen. They show only when printed, and only if your printer is capable of printing the enhancement. Unless equipped with certain graphics hardware, italic print will appear underlined on the screen and may also appear underlined when printed.

Whether enhancements appear on the screen or when printed depends upon the capability of your hardware.

GENERAL PROCEDURES

EMBEDDED COMMANDS

To Underline

- Bring a document to the screen.
- Decide which word, words, or line to underline.
- Move the cursor under the first letter to be underlined.
- Press <Alt>-<U>.
- Move the cursor to the space following the last letter to be underlined.
- Press <Alt>-<U>.

This is underlined text.

To Draw a Line

- Move cursor to where line is to begin.
- Press <Alt>-<U>.
- Hold down <Space Bar> to draw line.
- Hold <Ctrl> and press <Space Bar> to insert a hard space at the end of the line. The hard space character (a dot) will not be printed.
- Press <Alt>-<U>.

The line drawn can be empty or contain an entry. Here is an example which contains an entry (Date of Birth):

Date of Birth: _____

A line can also be drawn by pressing <Shift>-<Alt> and holding down <G> until the desired line length is achieved. Here is an example:

_____

To Boldface

- Bring a document to the screen.
- Decide which word, words, or line to boldface.
- Move the cursor under the first letter to be boldfaced.
- Press <Alt>-<B>.
- Move the cursor to the space following the last letter to be boldfaced.
- Press <Alt>-<B>.

This is boldface text

To Enlarge

- Bring a document to the screen.
- Decide which word, words, or line to enlarge.
- Move the cursor under the first letter to be enlarged.
- Press <Alt>-<D>.
- Move the cursor to the space following the last letter to be enlarged.
- Press <Alt>-<D>.

This is enlarged text

To Reduce

- Bring a document to the screen.
- Decide which word, words, or line to reduce.
- Move the cursor under the first letter to be reduced.
- Press <Alt>-<C>.
- Move the cursor to the space following the last letter to be reduced.
- Press <Alt>-<C>.

This is reduced text

To Enclose

- Bring a document to the screen.
- Decide which text to enclose in a box.
- Use the figures and keys shown in Figure 9-1 to draw the box.

To Draw These Figures	Use These Keys
(upper left corner)	Press \<Shift>-\<Alt>-\<Q>
(upper right corner)	Press \<Shift>-\<Alt>-\<E>
(lower left corner)	Press \<Shift>-\<Alt>-\<Z>
(lower right corner)	Press \<Shift>-\<Alt>-\<C>
(horizontal line)	Press \<Shift>-\<Alt>-\<G>
(vertical line)	Press \<Shift>-\<Alt>-\<V>

FIGURE 9-1 FIGURES AND KEY COMBINATIONS FOR DRAWING BOXES

GUIDED ACTIVITY 1 ENHANCING A DOCUMENT WITH EMBEDDED COMMANDS

1. Bring the file BALANCE.DOC to the screen. This file was created as part of Guided Activities 1 and 3, Unit 4; and Application D, Unit 6. Any of these three versions can be used for this guided activity. However, the Application D version is preferred, and it is the one upon which Figures 9-2 and 9-3 are based. If you are using a Unit 4 version of BALANCE.DOC, then the headers, footnotes, and page numbers will not appear, and you should proceed without them.

2. If not already present, embed a permannent ruler line with margins at 15 (L) and 65 (R).

3. Use the procedures described in this unit and produce the document shown in Figure 9-2.

4. Save the document under the file name BALANCE.G91. Follow this procedure:

   Press **F1**.
   Press **F5**.
   Type **BALANCE.G91** and press **\<Enter>**.
   Press **F1**.
   Press **F3**.

5. If not already present, insert a page break on the line "Examples of Liabilities are:" or "Examples of Capital are."

6. Print the document.

   If the name and date lines in small print are not centered when printed, return to the file and adjust the spacing to achieve centered printing.

7. Quit PC-Write.

This guided activity is completed.

Checkpoint

In addition to boldfacing, how would you also underline "balance" sheet" in the first paragraph? Write the actual sequence of characters on the line below.

Checkpoint

Look at your answer to the above checkpoint. Verify that the *same* font enhancement character appears at the beginning and the end of the text. If this is the case, then the enhancement characters have been properly "nested." If this is not the case, write the corrected version here.

The Balance Sheet

A DESCRIPTION OF A
BALANCE SHEET

Prepared by: (type your name here)
(insert the current date here)

A **balance sheet** shows the result of operating a
company over a given period of time. The time
period is usually one year.   A balance sheet has
<u>three</u> parts: **assets**, **liabilities**, and **capital**.

Assets are valuable things owned by the company.
Liabilities are debts owed by the company to
banks and claims against it by suppliers
(trade creditors). **Capital** is the amount of
the company's assets (after paying all
liabilities) that would be divided among
owners if the company were sold or went out of
business.

The balance sheet is important because it shows how
well a company is operating. It shows the
proportion of all the company's assets owned by or
owed to its trade creditors, banks, and owners. <u>If</u>
<u>the proportion owned by owners <1> increases, the</u>
<u>company is doing well</u>.

Examples of assets are:

- Bank accounts

- Accounts payable (amounts due from customers)

- Inventories

- Property, plant, and equipment

- Copyrights and patents

----
1. A company can have one owner (a sole
   proprietorship), several owners (a partnership),
   or many owners (a corporation).
      1

FIGURE 9-2 BALANCE.G91 (Page 1 only), THE RESULT OF GUIDED ACTIVITY 1

GLOBAL DOT COMMANDS

To Underline

- Bring a document to the screen.
- Decide which block of text to underline.
- Move the cursor to the left margin above the text. The margin can be either column 1 or the left ruler line margin.
- Press <Alt>-<G> to enter the guide line font character, and then type this dot line: .R:U
- Move the cursor to the left margin below the text. The margin can be column one or the margin set by the ruler line.
- Press <Alt>-<G> to enter the guide line font character, and then type this dot line: .Q:U

To Boldface

- Bring a document to the screen.
- Decide which block of text to make bold.
- Move the cursor to the left margin above the text. The margin can be column one or the margin set by the ruler line.
- Press <Alt>-<G> to enter the guide line font character, and then type this dot line: .R:B
- Move the cursor to the left margin below the text. The margin can be column one or the margin set by the ruler line.
- Press <Alt>-<G> to enter the guide line font character, and then type this dot line: .Q:B

To Enlarge

- Bring a document to the screen.
- Decide which block of text to enlarge.
- Move the cursor to the left margin above the text. The margin can be column one or the margin set by the the ruler line.
- Press <Alt>-<G> to enter the guide line font character, and then type this dot line: .R:D
- Move the cursor to the left margin below the text. The margin can be column one or the margin set by the ruler line.
- Press <Alt>-<G> to enter the guide line font character, and then type this dot line: .Q:D

To Reduce

- Bring a document to the screen.
- Decide which block of text to reduce.

- Move the cursor to the left margin above the text. The margin can be column one or the margin set by the ruler line.
- Press <Alt>-<G> to enter the guide line font character, and then type this dot line: .R:C
- Move the cursor to the left margin below the text. The margin can be column one or the margin set by the ruler line.
- Press <Alt>-<G> to enter the guide line font character, and then type this dot line: .Q:C

ENHANCEMENT POINTERS

Remember that dot line commands must not appear on the same line with text. Dot line commands must appear on separate lines.

More than one enhancement may be used for the same portion of text. For example, text can be both underlined and boldfaced. Not all enhancements can be used together. It depends on your printer. The enhancement characters must be properly nested.

Enhancement characters used within a box drawn with the characters shown in Figure 9-1 may not print properly and may cause the box lines to be misaligned.

Embedded enhancement characters will appear on the screen. When they do so, they seem to offset the spacing of text. Despite this, the text will print properly. To "hide" enhancement characters, hold down <Alt> and press <Space Bar>. To restore characters to the screen, press the same two keys.

Enhancement characters will not be interpreted when printed from DOS. For enhancements to be printed correctly, they must be printed using the PC-Write print program. This program was placed on your working disk in Unit 2.

Application

Bring the file BALANCE.G91 to the screen. Use F5 to rename the file BALANCE.A9G (see Guided Activity 1, Step 5, Unit 9). Enter enhancement commands and produce the document shown in Figure 9-3. Equivalent headings on page 2 should also be boxed. The items listed under each box heading should be boldfaced through the use of dot line commands. For page two of the document, boldface the equation that appears at the end of the last paragraph.

If the enlarged title heading and reduced name and date lines are not centered when printed, return to the file and adjust the spacing to achieve centered spacing.

The Balance Sheet

A DESCRIPTION OF A
BALANCE SHEET

Prepared by: (type your name here)
(insert the current date here)

A **balance sheet** shows the result of operating a company over a given period of time.   The time period is usually one year.   A balance sheet has three parts: **assets**, **liabilities**, and **capital**.

Assets are valuable things owned by the company. **Liabilities** are debts owed by the company to banks and claims against it by suppliers (trade creditors).   **Capital** is the amount of the company's assets (after paying all liabilities) that would be divided among owners if the company were sold or went out of business.

The balance sheet is important because it shows how well a company is operating. It shows the proportion of all the company's assets owned by or owed to its trade creditors, banks, and owners. If the proportion owned by owners <1> increases, the company is doing well.

Examples of assets

- **Bank accounts**

- **Accounts payable (amounts due from customers)**

- **Inventories**

- **Property, plant, and equipment**

- **Copyrights and patents**

----
1. A company can have one owner (a sole
   proprietorship), several owners (a partnership),
   or many owners (a corporation).

1

FIGURE 9-3 BALANCE.A9G (Page 1 only), THE RESULT OF APPLICATION G

REVIEW QUESTIONS

1. What are some of the purposes of enhancing text?

_____

_____

_____

_____

_____

2. Explain what is wrong with the statement "It's good to use a lot of enhancements."

_____

_____

_____

_____

_____

3. Identify five popular enhancements.

_____

_____

_____

_____

_____

4. What is the difference between embedded enhancements and global enhancements?

_____

_____

_____

5. List the procedure for bolfacing a block of text.

_____

_____

_____

_____

_____

DOCUMENTATION RESEARCH

Consult the PC-Write manual on the topic of the PRINT.TST file. summarize your findings, and record the page numbers for reference.

_____

_____

_____

_____

Consult the PC-Write manual on the topic of enhancements. List ten enhancements that PC-Write supports. Do not include enhancements discussed in Unit 9.

_____

_____

_____

_____

_____

_____

_____

3

ADVANCED WORD PROCESSING OPERATIONS

Unit 10 discusses the use of windows to look at different parts of the same document or parts of two documents at the same time, and to copy text from one document to another. Also discussed in Unit 10 is how to insert a whole document into another document, and how to integrate spreadsheets and databases into a document.

Unit 11 provides instructions on merging one document with another document to produce a third document. Such procedures can save time in producing the merged document. Detailed instructions on how to conduct a mail merge are presented.

10 INTEGRATED OPERATIONS: WINDOWS AND FILE INSERTION

LEARNING OBJECTIVES

Upon completion of this unit you should know how to

1. open windows in a document.

2. open windows to a second document.

3. view and copy text through windows.

4. insert one document into another document.

5. insert a spreadsheet or database into a document.

UNIT OUTLINE

Learning Objectives

Unit Outline

Introduction

Windows

File Insertion

General Procedures

    Windows in One Document

        To View Another Part of the Same Document

    Windows in Two Documents

        To View Two Documents at the Same Time

        To Copy From One Document to Another Document

    File Insertion

        To Insert One Document into Another Document

        To Insert a Spreadsheet or a Database into a Document

Application H

Review Questions

Documentation Research

INTRODUCTION

WINDOWS

Normally the PC-Write screen shows one document. You can show a second document by dividing the screen in half and displaying separate documents in each half. Each half of the screen is called a **window**. You can also have windows that view different parts of the same document.

Windows divide the screen horizontally. Windows are useful for copying a portion of one document to another part of the same document; editing one part of a document while using another part of the same document as a reference; copying a portion of one document into another document; and editing one document while using another document as a reference. Only two windows can appear at one time.

Windows are created and used by means of the ruler line and the ruler line menu. Figure 10-1 shows the ruler line menu.

Esc F1:Help F2.Clear F3:To-File F4.Insert F5.Default F6:From-file Grey- Col.60

FIGURE 10-1 THE WINDOW (RULER LINE) MENU

Pressing F2 in the edit mode brings the ruler line, and its associated menu, shown above, to the screen. When windows are on the screen, pressing F2 causes the cursor to jump back to the ruler line. Pressing F6 allows a different file to be brought into one of the windows.

FILE INSERTION

To **copy** text from one file to another means to send or insert a *portion* of one file into another. To **import** a file means to send or insert one *whole* file into another file. In both cases, the receiving file is altered, because it now contains additional text. The sending or inserted file is unchanged.

Copying is not limited to text files. Whole spreadsheet and database files, or portions of them, can also be copied into a document file. These features are covered in this unit.

GENERAL PROCEDURES

WINDOWS IN ONE DOCUMENT

To View Another Part of the Same Document

To open a window in a document, proceed as follows:

- Bring a document to the screen.
- Place the cursor where you want the screen to be divided.
- Press F2.
- Press <Up Arrow>.
- Edit the text in the top window.
- Press F2.
- Press (down Arrow).
- Edit the text in the bottom window.
- Press F2.
- Press F2.
- edit the windowless document.

Here is what happens on the screen:

Placing the cursor where you want the screen to be divided (usually around the middle of the screen) and pressing F2 divides the screen into two parts.

Pressing <Up Arrow> moves the cursor off the ruler line into the top window. The top window can now be edited. The normal edit status line is present. Any changes made can be saved. The bottom window is frozen.

Pressing F2 causes the cursor to move to the ruler line.

Pressing <Down Arrow> causes the cursor to move off the ruler line into the bottom window. The bottom window can now be edited. The normal edit status line is present. Changes made during editing can be saved. The top window is frozen.

Pressing F2 moves the cursor to the ruler line. Pressing F2 again removes the ruler line and the windows from the screen. You can now continue editing.

Figure 10-2 shows a screen with windows.

GUIDED ACTIVITY 1 OPENING WINDOWS IN A DOCUMENT

1. Bring the file **DECLARA.DOC** to the screen.

2. Place the cursor at the middle of the screen, press **F2**, and press **<Up Arrow>**.

3. Explore the document in the top window by pressing **<Up Arrow>** and **<Down Arrow>**.

4. Press **F2** to jump back to the ruler line and press **<Down Arrow>**.

5. Explore the document in the bottom window by pressing **<Up Arrow>** and **<Down Arrow>**.

6. Press **F2** to jump back to the ruler line.

7. Press **F2** to remove the ruler line, and the windows, from the screen.

This guided activity is completed.

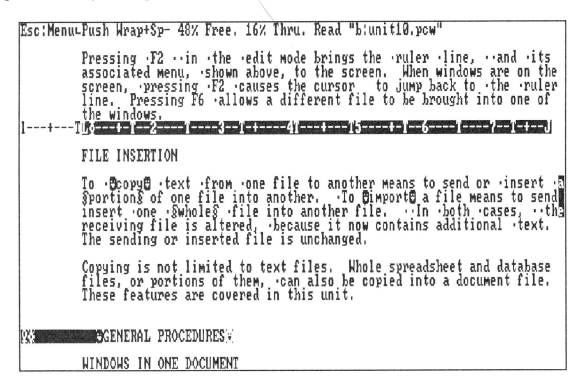

FIGURE 10-2 A SCREEN WITH WINDOWS

WINDOWS IN TWO DOCUMENTS

To View Two Documents at the Same Time

To open windows into different documents and copy text from one to another, proceed as follows:

- Bring a document to the screen.
- Place the cursor where you want the screen to be divided.
- Press F2 to display the ruler line.
- Press <Up Arrow>

The cursor moves into the top window. This is the window in which the second document will appear. Pressing <Down Arrow> would have selected the bottom window for the new document.

- Press F1 to display the System menu. One of its choices is F6:File.
- Press F6. The top line shows:

File to load or create (Esc:cancel F8:dir): "b:<filename>"

- Type the file name of the second document. You can either recall an existing document or create a new one.
- Press <Enter>, then press <Esc>.

The second document appears in the top window. There are now two separate documents on the screen. The cursor is in the top window. You can now edit one document while using the other as a reference.

To move from one window to the other, press F2 and then <Up Arrow>, or <Down Arrow>, as appropriate.

To remove the top window, move the cursor to the bottom window, and press F2 twice. To remove the bottom window, move the cursor to the top window, and press F2 twice.

To Copy From One Document to Another Document

You can copy text from one document to another. To copy text from the top window document to the bottom window document, proceed as follows:

- Establish windows in two documents as described above.
- Move the cursor to the top window.

- Move the cursor to the beginning of the text to be copied and press F3.
- Move the cursor to the end of the text to be copied and press F3.
- Press F2 to move the cursor onto the ruler line.
- Press <Down Arrow> to move the cursor into the bottom window.
- Move the cursor to the insert location.
- Press <Ctrl>-F4 to copy the text from the top window document to the bottom window document.
- Press F5 to unmark the text.
- Press F1, then F3 to save the change.
- Continue editing.

Note: See Unit 6 for copying a block of text from one document to another document without using windows.

GUIDED ACTIVITY 2   OPENING WINDOWS IN TWO DOCUMENTS

PART 1 WINDOWS IN DIFFERENT DOCUMENTS

1. Bring the file **COLUMBUS.DOC** to the screen.

2. Place the cursor in the middle of the screen.

3. Press **F2** and press **<Up Arrow>**.

4. Press **F1** then **F6** and type **POPUL.DOC**, the name of the second document.

5. Press **<Enter>** and notice that the second document appears in the top window.

6. Proceed to Part 2.

PART 2 COPYING FROM ONE DOCUMENT TO ANOTHER

In this part we will copy text from the top window document to the bottom window document.

1. Move the cursor to beginning of the first paragraph and press **F3**.

2. Move cursor to the end of the first paragraph and press **F3**.

3. Press **F2** to move the cursor to the ruler line.

4. Press **<Down Arrow>** to move the cursor to the bottom window.

5. Move cursor two lines below the last line in the document and press **<Ctrl>-F4** to copy the text from the document in the top window to the document in the bottom window.

6. Press **F5** to unmark the text.

7. Save and print the document in the bottom window.

This guided activity is completed.

Checkpoint

How is a window removed from the screen?

_____

_____

FILE INSERTION

To Insert One Document Into Another Document

To insert all the text from one document into a document you are currently editing, proceed as follows:

- Bring a document to the screen.
- Move the cursor to where you want the file to be inserted.
- Press (Ctrl)-F3. The top line reads:

   File to insert (Esc: Cancel F8: dir): "<filename>"

- Type a file name or call up the directory by pressing F8 and select a filename.
- Press <Enter> to insert the entire document at the cursor.
- Press F5 to unmark the inserted document.
- Continue editing.

GUIDED ACTIVITY 3   INSERTING ONE DOCUMENT INTO ANOTHER DOCUMENT

In this activity *all* the text from one document is inserted into another document.

1. Create a file describing the most enjoyable college course you have taken, or are now taking. Include at least three specific reasons for identifying this course as the most enjoyable.

2. Create another file describing the least enjoyable college course you have taken, or are now taking. Include at least three specific reasons for identifying this course as least enjoyable.

3. Use the procedure described above under "To Insert One Document Into Another Document", and insert the first document into the second document.

4. Save and print the combined document.

5. Analyze the text associated with the most enjoyable course. Based on this analysis, reenter the file and add a paragraph describing two things you might have done during the least-liked course to make it more enjoyable.

6. Save and print the document.

This guided activity is completed.

To Insert a Spreadsheet or Database Into a Document

Other types of files besides document files can be inserted in a PC-Write document. For example, you can insert a database or spreadsheet file.

The file to be inserted should be in ASCII format; or, it should have been created using the other program's print-to-disk feature.

To insert a file from a spreadsheet or database program, you will need that program's System disk and an associated data file.

- Bring a document to the screen.
- Press F1, then F4, and press <Enter> to return to the DOS A> prompt.
- Bring an actual spreadsheet or database to the screen.
- Press <Shift>-<Ctrl>-F5 to clear the memory hold area of any text it may contain.
- Press <Shift>-<Ctrl>-F6 and move the cursor to the beginning of the material to be inserted.
- Press <Shift>-<Ctrl>-F6 and move the cursor to the end of the material to be inserted.
- Press <Shift>-<Ctrl>-F6 to copy the material to the computer's memory hold area.
- Quit the spreadsheet or database and return to the A> prompt.
- Type EXIT at the A> prompt to return to PC-Write.
- Press <Ctrl>-F4 to place the contents of the hold area in the document.
- Continue editing the document.

An entire spreadsheet or database file can be inserted in a document by "clipping" all of it as described above, or by importing the total file as described above under "To Insert One Document In Another Document." However, either the whole spreadsheet or database file to be imported must be in ASCII format or the file should be created using the spreadsheet's or database's print-to-disk feature.

Application

PART 1   INSERTING A SPREADSHEET INTO A DOCUMENT

For this application you will need a Lotus 123, Version 2 Systems disk. A spreadsheet file (CLIP.WK1) is already on your data disk.

If you do not have Lotus 123 software, you may use any other spreadsheet program that is compatible with PC-DOS. Use that program to create the spreadsheet shown inside the box in Figure 10-3, or use another, existing, spreadsheet. If you use a spreadsheet program other than Lotus 123, make the appropriate substitutions in the steps that follow.

If you are using a floppy disk system, The following procedure assumes that your spreadsheet program is configured to access drive B for data files.

Figure 10-3 shows the result of this application.

Create the file **CLIP.DOC**, and embed a permanent ruler line with margins at 15 (L) and 65 (R). Type in the material shown above the box in Figure 10-3.

Perform the following steps:

a. Press **F1**, then **F4**, and press **<Enter>** to return to the DOS A> prompt

b. Insert the Lotus System disk in Drive A, type **123** at the A> prompt , and press **<Enter>**.

c. Tap the following keys: **/ F R** Use **<Right Arrow>** to highlight the file name **CLIP.WK1**, and press **<Enter>**. The spreadsheet file CLIP.WK1 should now be on the screen

d. Press **<Shift>-<Ctrl>-F5** to clear the memory hold area of any text it may contain.

e. Press **<Shift>-<Ctrl>-F6** and move the cursor to the "S" in "Summary."

f. Press **<Shift>-<Ctrl>-F6** and move the cursor to the "1" in "81."

g. Press **<Shift>-<Ctrl>-F6** to copy the spreadsheet material to the memory hold area.

h. Tap the following keys: **/ Q Y** to return to the DOS A> prompt.

i. Type **EXIT** at the A> prompt to return to PC-Write.

j. Press **<Ctrl>-F4** to place the contents of the hold area in the document. Press F5 to unmark the text.

k. Use Figure 10-3 as a guide to center the spreadsheet, draw a box around it, and type the material below the box. Add your name and the current date at the bottom of the document.

l. Save and print the document.

PC-Write's SCREEN CLIP FEATURE

PC-Write's Screen Clip feature allows the insertion of material from another **program** into a PC-Write document.

For example, if you are writing a document and want to include part of a Lotus 123 spreadsheet in your document you can:

- Exit your PC-Write document
- Load 123
- Mark the spreadsheet cells you want to bring into your document
- Leave 123
- Re-enter your PC-Write document and place the spreadsheet cells where you want it

The material inside the box shown below was imported from a Lotus 123 Rel.2 spreadsheet. Imported material can be editied just like any other text. The box was drawn around the spreadsheet cells after it was imported and moved to the center of this document .

Summary of PC-Write's Main Menu Commands		
Main Menu Name	Number of Main Commands	Associated Sub Commands
Esc	10	26
Alt	7	32
Shift	6	16
Ctrl	7	7
Totals	30	81

Material Imported From a Lotus 123 Spreadsheet

See the discussion in this unit for the detailed procedure for using the Screen Clip feature.

FIGURE 10-3 CLIP.DOC, THE RESULT OF PART 1, APPLICATION H

PART 2   INSERTING A DATABASE INTO A DOCUMENT

Use an available database software package and prepare a database file which contains the following type of data on each of ten family members or friends:

First Name
Last Name
Age
Weight in pounds
Height on inches

Write a memorandum (see Appendix C for a memorandum format) from you to your instructor which describes the hobbies, interests, or jobs of each person in your file. Insert the database into the document and identify it as additional information about each person. Print the document.

PART 3 COMBINING DOCUMENT FILES

Use the window technique to combine the three document files listed below. The files are on your data disk.

BF.DOC
POPUL.DOC
DECLARA.DOC

Create an appropriate title for the combined document. Print the title in enlarged print. Add appropriate boldfaced sub-titles at the beginning of each document section. Boldface all names that appear in the combined document. Insert page breaks. Create an appropriate header. Print page numbers along the bottom. Save and print the document.

REVIEW QUESTIONS

1. What is a document window?

_____

_____

2. Identify four reasons for using a document window.

_____

_____

_____

_____

3. What is the procedure for establishing a window in a document?

_____

_____

_____

_____

_____

_____

_____

_____

_____

4. What is the window procedure to copy text from one document to another document?

_____

_____

_____

_____

_____

_____

_____

5. What is the procedure for copying a spreadsheet into a document?

_____

_____

_____

_____

_____

_____

_____

_____

_____

_____

DOCUMENTATION RESEARCH

Consult the PC-Write manual and determine how the window feature can be used to set a book-mark. Summarize your findings below.

_____

_____

_____

_____

11 INTEGRATED OPERATIONS: MERGING

LEARNING OBJECTIVES

Upon completion of this unit you should know how to

1. prepare an input file.

2. prepare a document file.

3. merge an input file with a document file.

4. print merged documents.

UNIT OUTLINE

Learning Objectives

Unit Outline

Introduction

Merging Documents

General Procedure

The Input File With Names and Addresses

    Records and Fields

    Record Variations

The Document File Containing The Form Letter and Merge Instructions

    Field Names

    The Form Letter and Field Names

    General Merge Rules to Follow

        The Document

        The Field Names Above the Single, Empty Set of Curly Brackets

        The Field Names Below the Single, Empty Set of Curly Brackets

Execution of the Merge Operation

Printing Merged Documents

Application I

Review Questions

Documentation Research

INTRODUCTION

This unit discusses how to bring two documents together in a systematic manner to create a third document. Bringing two documents together to produce a third is called **merging**.

Systematically adding a name and address from one document to a sales letter document, for the purpose of producing a third document each with a different name and address but with the same letter, is an example of merging.

MERGING DOCUMENTS

Suppose you want to send the same sales letter to a number of people on a list. You could bring the letter to the screen, type in a name and address at the beginning of the letter, and print the letter. You could then repeat the process, again and again, for all the remaining people on your list.

Such an operation is called **merging**. You have merged your name list with a standard sales form letter to produce a series of letters, each addressed to a different person. However, the manual approach to merging is time consuming and error prone. PC-Write can perform a merge in less time and with less chance of error.

GENERAL PROCEDURE

Here is the general procedure for producing merged documents such as the mail merge described above:

- Create an input file with names and addresses.
- Create a document file containing the form letter and merge instructions.
- Execute the merge operation.
- Print the merged documents.

The following sections addresses each of these four steps.

THE INPUT FILE WITH NAMES AND ADDRESSES

The input file is a regular PC-Write text file. It starts in the upper left-hand corner of the screen, row 1, column 1. Here is a sample file which separates information by commas:

```
Mr.,John Adams,27 Berry Drive,New York, NY,10017
Mr.,Benjamin Franklin,"Spectator Ave., NW",Philadelphia,PA,12345
Ms.,Betsy Ross,1300 Flag Road,Philadelphia,PA,12345
,John Hart,Roads Way,Trenton, NJ,07632
Dr.,William Hart Ellery,Apple Orchard Road,
Upton,Rhode Island,21354
Prof.,Wm. Floyd,North Way,Flanders,NY,""
Sir,John Morton,Bent Path,Ridgefield,CT,06877
```

As you read the following material, refer to the input file listed above and observe the point being made.

RECORDS AND FIELDS

Each line of information for an individual person is called a **record**.

Each separate piece of information in a record is called a **field**.

Although the amount of information in each record varies in length, the following standard field format is followed for each person:

[title] [name] [street address] [city] [state] [zip]

To simplify this discussion, we will assume that each record will have the same number of fields.

Each field is separated by a comma.

In the example shown, the input file has seven records, each with six fields.

RECORD VARIATIONS

The second record contains quotation marks around the third field (street address) because that field includes a comma. The quotation marks tell PC-Write that the comma is actually part of the field information and not to interpret it as a field separator. The double quotation mark, not the single quotation mark, must be used.

The fourth record starts with a comma because the first field in that record is to be left empty. If the state field were also missing, the record would look like this:

,John Hart,Roads Way,Trenton,,07632

The fifth record is continued on a second line because the first line ends with a comma.

The sixth record has an empty last field. The two quotation marks at the end signify the end of the record. Otherwise (since the record ends with a comma), the seventh record would be interpreted as being part of the sixth record. Why not simply leave off the last comma and the quotation marks? The sixth record would not then have six fields and all records must have the same number of fields.

The maximum field length in PC-Write is 160 characters.

The input file can have any number of records (limited only by disk space).

GUIDED ACTIVITY 1   CREATING AN INPUT FILE

1. Get PC-Write ready. Type **ED B:NAME.LST** to create a new file.

2. Carefully type the following records into the file. Start at the first line, first column, at the top of the screen.

> Mr.,John Adams,27 Berry Drive,New York, NY,10017 _Record #1_
> Mr.,Benjamin Franklin,"Spectator Ave., NW",Philadelphia,PA,12345
> Ms.,Betsy Ross,1300 Flag Road,Philadelphia,PA,12345
> ,John Hart,Roads Way,Trenton, NJ,07632
> Dr.,William Hart Ellery,Apple Orchard Road,
> Upton,Rhode Island,21354
> Prof.,Wm. Floyd,North Way,Flanders,NY,""
> Sir,John Morton,Bent Path,Ridgefield,CT,06877

3. Press **F1**, then **F2** to save the file and quit PC-Write.

This guided activity is completed.

THE DOCUMENT FILE CONTAINING THE FORM LETTER AND MERGE INSTRUCTIONS

The document file is a regular PC-Write text file. It has two parts: a field names part and a form letter part. Here is a sample document file.

```
{title,}
{name,}
{address,}
{city,}
{state,}
{zip,}
{}
{title} {name}
{address}
{city} {state} {zip}

Dear {title} {name}

    Take advantage {title+} {name+} of our special offer to all
residents of {city+}.

    Purchase our vacuum cleaner, {title+} {name+}, by July 2, 1990
and we will deliver it to your home at {address+} at the special
price of $99.95.


Sincerely,

I. Sellum
Sales Manager

(on this line press <ALT>-T then <ALT>-G then type two dots (periods))
```

FIELD NAMES

Everything above the single, empty set of curly brackets represents a name for each field in a record. The names are then used in the form letter to tell PC-Write where in the form letter to place the actual field information.

THE FORM LETTER AND FIELD NAMES

Everything below the single, empty set of curly brackets represents the form letter. The form letter contains embedded instructions inside the curly brackets.

Here is how the merge works:

When the first record in the input file is processed, the following field name matchups are made. These matchups are based upon the field name layout *above* the single, empty set of curly brackets.

Actual Field Value in Record:	Assigned to Field Name:
Mr.	{title,}
John Adams	{name,}
27 Berry Drive	{address,}
New York	{city,}
NY	{state,}
10017	{zip,}

Now, every time PC-Write sees a field name in the form letter, it interprets it as an instruction to substitute the actual field value. When it sees "{title,}" in the form letter, it substitutes "Mr."; when it sees "{name,}" it substitutes "John Adams"; and so on, until all substitutions for a given record have been made.

When the next record is processed, its field values are substituted for the field names in the form letter. This procedure continues until all records have been processed and a separate letter has been created for each record in the file. A separate file containing the merged letters is created during this process.

GENERAL MERGE RULES TO FOLLOW

The Document

The form letter part must come *after* the field names part.

The two parts *must* be separated by a single, empty set of curly brackets.

The Field Names Above the Single, Empty Set of Curly Brackets

Do not put blank spaces in field names.

The field names inside the curly brackets must end with a comma.

The Field Names Below the Single, Empty Set of Curly Brackets

Field names must appear exactly the same as those above the single, empty set of curly brackets, however:

Do not use trailing commas below the single, empty set of curly brackets.

Since merging turns off reformatting, include a + sign after the field name to turn reformatting on.

Field names can be placed anywhere in the form letter.

GUIDED ACTIVITY 2 CREATING A DOCUMENT FILE

1. Create the file **SALESLTR.DOC**.

2. Type the following into the file. Start at the first line at the top of the screen.

>   {title,}
>   {name,}
>   {address,}
>   {city,}
>   {state,}
>   {zip,}
>   {}
>   {title} {name}
>   {address}
>   {city} {state} {zip}
>
>   Dear {title} {name}
>
>   Take advantage, {title+} {name+}, of our special offer to all residents of {city+}.
>
>   Purchase our vacuum cleaner, {title+} {name+}, by July 2, 1990 and we will deliver it to your home at {address+} at the special price of $99.95.
>
>
>   Sincerely
>
>   I. Sellum
>   Sales Manager

On this line press **<ALT>-T**, then **<ALT>-G**, then type two dots.

3. Press **F1**, then **F2** to save the file and quit PC-Write.

This guided activity is completed.

EXECUTION OF THE MERGE OPERATION

Once the input file and the document file have been created, the files can be merged and stored or merged and printed. Here is the general procedure for performing the merge.

- Press <Shift> F2 _[F3]_. The Merge menu appears:

Esc F1 F5. Edit F6.Stop F7.Input F8.Output F9:Files F10.Repeat. Next-record:1

- Press F9. The top line shows this:

Esc F8:Dir F9:Input "merge.lst" F10: "merge.out"

The cursor is at the Input file name. "merge.lst" is the default file name for the input name and address file. "merge.out" is the default file name for the output file which will contain the merged letters. For this discussion, let's assume that the name and address file name is "name.lst" and that the output letter file name is "Letters.out."

- Type "name.lst" as the input file name.
- Press F10. The cursor moves to the output file name. You now have two choices:

   a) Enter "prn" as the output file name and the merged documents will be printed directly, OR,

   b) Enter "letters.out" as the output file name and the merged documents will be sent to a disk file called "letters.out." This file (which contains all the merged documents) can then be printed by first loading it with the ED command. Or, it can be printed directly from the DOS prompt with the PR command.

      Note: If your document file contains a form letter with font or dot line characters in the body of the letter, you must choose the second option. This will allow such characters to be interpreted by the PC-Write print (PR) program. For this discussion, we will assume option 2.

- Type "letters.out" for the output file name and press <Enter>.
- Press F7
  The first record is merged with the sales letter and displayed on the screen. These options are now available:

   a) Verify or edit the document for corrections. To edit the document press F5 or <Esc>. When you have finished editing, press <Shift> F2 _[F3]_. The merge menu will return.

   b) Send the merged document to the disk output file (F8).

   c) Send a second copy of the merged document to the disk output file (F10).

all Shift F2 → Shift F3

    d) Do not send the merged document to the disk output file. In other words, skip the record (F7).

    e) Merge another record (F7).

    f) Merge the remaining records automatically (F10).

    g) Stop merging (F6).

■ Press F8.
The merged document is sent to the output file.

It is a good practice to verfify one more merged record and then have the remaining records merged automatically.

■ Press F7.
The second record is merged with the sales letter and displayed on the screen.

■ Press F8.
The second merged letter is sent to the disk output file.

■ Press F10.
This automatically "presses" F7 and F8 until all input file records have been processed and sent to the disk output file.

When the merge is complete the top line shows this: "All input file records merged normally." The document file returns to the screen.

■ Quit PC-Write.

GUIDED ACTIVITY 3   EXECUTING THE MERGE OPERATION

1. Get PC-Write ready and bring **SALESLTR.DOC** to the screen.

2. Press **<Shift> F2**. The Merge menu appears:

Esc F1 F5. Edit F6.Stop F7.Input F8.Output F9:Files F10.Repeat. Next-record:1

3. Press **F9**. The Top Line shows this:

Esc F8:Dir F9:Input "merge.lst" F10: "merge.out"

The cursor is at the Input file name.

4. Type **B:NAME.LST**

5. Press **F10**; the cursor moves to the output file name.

6. Type: **B:LETTERS.OUT** and press **<Enter>**.

7. Press **F7**. Notice that the first record (John Adams) is merged with the sales letter and displayed on the screen.

8. Verify that the merged document is correct by inspecting the placement of the field values. If correct, proceed to step 9. If incorrect, press F5, correct the document, and press <Shift>-F2 F3 to return to the merge menu. Proceed to step 9.

9. Press **F8** to send the merged document to the output file.

10. You will verify one more merged record and then have the remaining records merged automatically.

11. Press **F7** and notice that the second record (Benjamin Franklin) is merged with the sales letter and displayed on the screen. Verify the document.

12. Press **F8** to send the second merged document to the disk output file.

13. Press **F10** to automatically "press" F7 and F8, to process all input records, and send them to the disk output file.

14. Notice the top line shows "All input file records merged normally". The document file is on the screen.

15. Quit PC-Write.

This guided activity is completed.

Checkpoint

If you do not supply a file name for the file that holds the merged documents, what file name does PC-Write use?

PRINTING MERGED DOCUMENTS

Now that an output file containing the merged documents has been created, the merged documents can be printed.

- Bring the DOS A> prompt to the screen.
- Verify that the PC-Write working disk is in drive A and the data disk (containing the output file with the merged documents) is in drive B.
- Type PR B:LETTERS.OUT and press <Enter>.
- Press F10 twice to print the merged documents.

GUIDED ACTIVITY 4 PRINTING THE MERGED DOCUMENTS

1. Get PC-Write ready.

2. Type **PR B:LETTERS.OUT** and press **<Enter>**.

3. Press **F10**.

4. Press **F10** to print the merged documents.

This guided activity is completed.

Application

PART 1 FRIEND FILE

a) Prepare an input file with the names and addresses of five of your friends.

b) Prepare a document file with a form letter inviting your friends to a party. The addressee's name should appear at least twice in the form letter.

c) Merge the input file with the document file.

d) Print the merged documents.

PART 2 OVERDUE BOOKS

You are a librarian with a name and address list of seven people whose books are overdue by 60 days or more. Each person has one book. Each book is a different number of days overdue.

Prepare a form letter to be sent to each person on the list. The form letter will request the return of the book. The letter should include a statement which shows the number of days the book is overdue.

Hint: In preparing the input file, include a field in each record which will hold the number of overdue days. Declare this field in the field names portion of the document, above the single, empty set of curly brackets. Then use the field names as required in the body of the form letter.

PART 3 UNPAID BILLS

You are a billing manager with a name and address list of customers with overdue outstanding balances. The list also includes the number of days each account is overdue, the amount overdue, and the date of last purchase.

Prepare a form letter to be sent to each person on the list. The letter should contain a summary area, just below the inside address, which lists the amount overdue, number of days overdue, and date of last purchase. The amount and days overdue should also be repeated and underlined in the body of the letter.

Hint: In preparing the input file, include fields in each record which will hold days overdue, amount overdue, and date of last purchase. Declare these fields in the field names portion of the document, above the single, empty set of curly brackets. Then use the field names as required in the body of the form letter.

REVIEW QUESTIONS

1. Describe in general terms the mail merge process.

   _____

   _____

   _____

2. List the four basic steps in a computer-based mail merge operation.

   _____

   _____

   _____

   _____

3. What is a record?

   _____

4. What is a field?

   _____

5. What, if anything, limits the number of records in a file?

   _____

6. What is the purpose of placing commas in input records?

   _____

7. Why can't a record end with a comma?

   _____

8. How can a comma be included as part of a field?

   _____

9. In the document file, what symbol is used to separate the field names portion of the file from the form letter portion of the file?

_____

10. Which symbols must appear at the end of the document file to assure each letter is printed on a separate page?

_____

11. How many times can a field name be used in the body of the form letter?

_____

12. How can reformatting be assured in a form letter?

13. What would happen if some of the fields that appear in an input record were not used in the form letter?

_____

DOCUMENTATION RESEARCH

Consult the PC-Write manual and determine the process for conducting a mail merge without an input file. Record your notes here.

_____

_____

_____

_____

_____

_____

GETTING STARTED ON YOUR MICROCOMPUTER

This appendix covers the knowledge necessary to use applications software and the Disk Operating System (DOS) with the IBM PC or compatible microcomputers. It is not intended to make you an expert in DOS, but to provide some level of competence by setting forth the necessary operations external to the software discussed in this manual.

PART 1 THE KEYBOARD

The IBM and other personal computers have over 80 keys, about 40 more than most type-writers. An illustration of the keyboard appears inside the back cover of this manual. Many of the "extra" keys have symbols or mnemonics rather than characters. To minimize confusion, the following conventions are used in THE MICROCOMPUTING SERIES.

Keys with multiple character names have those names spelled out, usually followed by the word *key*. Examples include *the F1 key*, *the Ins key*, *the Home key*, and *the Del key*. Keys with symbols only have the key name enclosed in < > signs:

<TAB>   Gray key just below the Esc key, marked with two arrows.

<SHIFT>   Gray keys: one between the Ctrl and Alt keys, the other just above the Caps Lock key, marked with hollow upward arrows.

<BACKSPACE>   Gray key in top row of keyboard with arrow pointing to the left.

<CR>   Gray key between the <BACKSPACE> and PrtSc keys, marked with bent arrow.

<ARROW KEYS>   White keys on the right of the keyboard, each marked with an arrow; also called <UP>, <LEFT>, <DOWN>, and <RIGHT>. Note that <LEFT> and <BACKSPACE> are different keys and perform different functions in most software packages.

We assume that you know how to use the <SHIFT> key to obtain an uppercase letter or a symbol character, and we do not explicitly mention the <SHIFT> in most cases.

FUNCTION KEYS

These ten keys are located in two columns along the left edge of the keyboard. Most application software packages make special use of these keys. Although these keys also have special meanings when used by DOS, we ignore those uses here to avoid confusion with the application program that is the subject of this manual.

MULTIPLE KEY COMBINATIONS

On a typewriter, <SHIFT> is used in conjunction with a letter key to produce a capital letter. The same is true on a computer. On a computer, the Ctrl and Alt keys also act as modifying keys; if either of these is used in conjunction with another key, the original meaning of the letter key is modified. These keys are manipulated in the same manner as <SHIFT>. For example, to enter Alt-M (sometimes written Alt + M), hold down the Alt key then press M.

TOGGLE KEY FUNCTIONS

Toggle keys act as on-off switches. Press a toggle key once and the function is activated, press it a second time and the function is deactivated. The toggle keys are the Num Lock key (which activates the numeric keypad), the Scroll Lock key (used in only a few software packages), the Ctrl-PrtSc combination (which directs screen display to the printer as well), and the Caps Lock key.

CAPS LOCK KEY

The Caps Lock key shifts all alphabetic (A . . . Z) characters to upper case, but has no effect on any other key. (This is unlike a typewriter, where the Shift Lock key changes numeric character keys to symbols.) The Caps Lock key is a toggle key. If you are typing in capital letters and need one or two lower case letters (such as in the word *McCLELLAN*), then pressing <SHIFT> plus the letter you wish in lower case will yield the desired effect.

NUMERIC KEYPAD KEYS

These are the keys on the right side of the keyboard arranged as a 10-key pad. The keys with arrows on them are referred to as <ARROW KEYS>, or as <UP>, <LEFT>, <RIGHT>, and <DOWN>. The other keys in this group are referred to by the text that appears on them: Home, PgUp, PgDn, End, Del, and Ins. The numeric function of the keys can be activated by using the Num Lock key (a toggle). Most of these keys have no effect when in DOS, but are used by many application programs to control movement on the screen.

PART 2 STARTUP AND SHUTDOWN PROCEDURES

LOADING DOS

Loading DOS means transferring some of the programs in the Disk Operating System from a *System Disk* into the computer's memory. You must load DOS before you can use any application software or any of the system's utilities.

Some application software requires you to use the DOS disk to load the system before using the application program disk. Other application software gives you instructions on how to install DOS onto the software program disk in order to make the software self-loading and provide some system functions without having to switch disks.

THE DOS PROMPT

The DOS or system prompt (A>_ with most floppy disk systems and C>_ with most hard disk systems) tells you that it is your turn to type information; that is, you must tell DOS what to do next by entering a command. The DOS prompt will appear on the screen after you have successfully loaded DOS. *Many of the command examples in this appendix show the DOS prompt, but you should not type the A> or C>, it has already been supplied by DOS.*

STARTUP PROCEDURES IF THE MICROCOMPUTER SYSTEM IS TURNED OFF

Floppy Disk Systems

1. Insert the DOS disk or a program disk on which DOS has been installed into Disk Drive A:. (This is the left-hand drive on IBM PCs. Your instructor or lab supervisor will tell you if otherwise on the equipment you are using.)

2. When the disk is fully inserted, close the drive door. You should not have to force the door closed; if the door is not closing easily, remove and reinsert the disk.

3. With a dual-disk system, insert the disk you will use for your data files into Disk Drive B:.

4. When the disk is fully inserted, close the drive door.

5. If a printer is attached to your computer, make sure that it is turned on and that the POWER, READY, and ON LINE lights (or their equivalent) are on.

6. Turn on the power switch. On IBM PCs, this is at the rear of the right side of the computer. On some other PCs, the power switch is on the rear of the computer. On some systems, you must also turn on the monitor (display screen) power switch.

7. When the red disk-in-use light goes off, DOS should be loaded. You may need to adjust the contrast and brightness controls on the monitor. In most cases, you will be asked to enter the date and time.

8. The next step is dependent upon specific software. For the DOS commands discussed in this appendix, leave the DOS disk in drive A:. For the software discussed in this manual, appropriate instructions are presented in Part 1.

Hard Disk Systems

1. If a printer is attached to your computer, make sure that it is turned on and that the POWER, READY, and ON LINE lights (or their equivalent) are on.

2. Turn on the power switch. On IBM PC/XTs, this is at the rear of the right side of the computer. On some other PCs, the power switch is on the rear of the computer. On some systems, you must also turn on the monitor (display screen) power switch.

3. When the red disk-in-use light goes off, DOS should be loaded. You may need to adjust the contrast and brightness controls on the monitor. In most cases, you will be asked to enter the date and time.

4. The next step is dependent upon specific software. For the DOS commands discussed in this appendix, you may place the disk you will use for your data files in the disk drive. For the software discussed in this manual, appropriate instructions are presented in Part 1.

STARTUP PROCEDURES IF THE MICROCOMPUTER SYSTEM IS TURNED ON

Floppy Disk Systems

1. Insert the DOS disk or a program disk on which DOS has been installed into Disk Drive A:. (This is the left-hand drive on IBM PCs, your instructor or lab supervisor will tell you if otherwise on the equipment you are using.) You may need to adjust the contrast and brightness controls on the monitor.

2. When the disk is fully inserted, close the drive door. You should not have to force the door closed; if the door is not closing easily, remove and reinsert the disk.

3. With a dual-disk system, insert the disk you will use for your data files into Disk Drive B:.

4. When the disk is fully inserted, close the drive door.

5. If a printer is attached to your computer, make sure that it is turned on and that the POWER, READY, and ON LINE lights (or their equivalent) are on.

6. Load (or reload) DOS by pressing and holding, in order, the Ctrl, the Alt, and the Del keys. After pressing Del, *release all three keys.*

7. When the red disk-in-use light goes off, DOS should be loaded. In most cases, you will be asked to enter the date and time.

8. The next step is dependent upon specific software. For the DOS commands discussed in this appendix, leave the DOS disk in drive A:. For the software discussed in this manual, appropriate instructions are presented in Part 1.

Hard Disk Systems

1. If a printer is attached to your computer, make sure that it is turned on and that the POWER, READY, and ON LINE lights (or their equivalent) are on. You may need to adjust the contrast and brightness controls on the monitor.

2. Load (or reload) DOS by pressing and holding, in order, the Ctrl, the Alt, and the Del keys. After pressing Del, *release all three keys.*

3. When the red disk-in-use light goes off, DOS should be loaded. In most cases, you will be asked to enter the date and time.

4. The next step is dependent upon specific software. For the DOS commands discussed in this appendix, you may place the disk you will use for your data files in the disk drive. For the software discussed in this manual, appropriate instructions are presented in Part 1.

SETTING THE DATE AND TIME

We strongly recommend that you set the date and time in the computer each time you begin a work session. This will allow the computer to *time stamp* your files so you will know when you last edited a file and, if you have the same file on many disks, which version of the file is most current. (Some microcomputers have a clock built in which will automatically set the time. If your system has this feature, the operating system disk will normally bypass the date and time queries and you may skip these procedures.)

When Loading DOS

The setting of the date and time at startup is illustrated in Figure App-1.

1. When DOS asks for the current date, type today's date using the following format: mm/dd/yy *or* mm-dd-yy, replacing mm with the number of the month (e.g., 03 for March), and so on. Press <CR> after entering the year number. *Do not type the name of the day, even though DOS will show you the name of the day.* If you make an entry that DOS does not recognize, an *invalid date* message will be displayed and you will be asked to reenter.

2. When DOS asks for the time, type the current time using the format hh:mm:ss.hs. (In most cases, hours and minutes -- hh:mm -- are sufficient; any number not entered is set to 0 [zero].) You must use the 24-hour clock, i.e., 10 A.M. is entered as **10**, while 1:25 P.M. is **13:25**. If you make an entry that DOS does not recognize, an *invalid time* message will be displayed and you will be asked to reenter.

```
Current date is Tue  1-01-1980
Enter new date: 3-22-86
Current time is  0:00:51.41
Enter new time: 12:40


The IBM Personal Computer DOS
Version 2.10 (C)Copyright IBM Corp 1981, 1982, 1983

A>_
```

FIGURE App-1 Setting the Date and Time at Startup
Note: Items entered by user are in **boldface.**

Resetting the Date

If you entered the wrong date or forgot to set the date when you started the system, you may reset the date with the DATE command:

1. Type **date** followed by <CR>.

2. Enter the appropriate date as discussed above.

Resetting the Time

If you entered the wrong time or forgot to set the time when you started the system, you may reset the time with the TIME command:

1. Type **time** followed by <CR>.

2. Enter the appropriate time as discussed above.

SHUTDOWN PROCEDURES

1. Make sure you have followed the proper escape or exit procedures for the software program you are using. Failure to follow such precautions may result in lost data.

2. When you have successfully exited the applications software or completed the last DOS command, you should have the command (A>__ or C>__) prompt.

3. Remove the disk(s) from the disk drive(s). Place the disk(s) in their protective jackets or other holders. *Do not shut the disk drive doors.*

4. Follow your organization's policy concerning turning the power off or leaving the system on. In general, it is advisable to leave the system on if someone else will be using it within a short amount of time; otherwise turn everything off. If you leave the system on, turn down the contrast control or type the DOS command **CLS** to protect the display screen.

PART 3 DOS COMMANDS

TO ISSUE COMMANDS

1. The command must be typed exactly as described in this appendix, including any spaces within the command.

2. Commands may be entered in uppercase or lowercase. DOS will convert them to uppercase.

3. Terminate all commands with <CR>.

4. If the command contains a typographical error, a missing space, or an extra space, the message *Bad command or file name* will appear after you press <CR>. If this happens, simply retype the command correctly. Many commands are disk files, and require that the DOS disk be present. If you get this message when you have not made a typographical error, check to see if the command is on the disk (using the DIR command discussed below).

TO CORRECT A TYPING MISTAKE BEFORE YOU PRESS <CR>

1. The <BACKSPACE> key may be used to correct errors made while in DOS. Characters will be erased as you backspace. The <LEFT ARROW> key has the same effect (in DOS). Once the mistaken character has been erased, type the proper character. If the remainder of the line (to the right of the error) was correct, press the <RIGHT ARROW> key to reinstate the characters. Otherwise, retype from the point of the correction.

2. If a line has many errors, you may prefer to press the Esc key, which will eliminate the line. A backslash (\ ) will appear and the cursor will move down one line. The line with errors may still appear on the screen, but it will not affect the command. You may now enter the corrected command.

TO STOP A COMMAND IN PROGRESS

1. Press the Ctrl key, then the Scroll Lock/Break key.

2. Release both keys; execution of the command will halt.

3. The system prompt (A>__ or C>__) will appear and the next command may be entered.

COMMAND AND FILE NAME PARAMETERS

Command and file names must be carefully entered into the system. Since most commands are special types of files, we can discuss parameters which apply to both *command names* and *file names*. Some parameters are required, and others are optional. If a parameter is omitted, the system will supply a default value. Upper- and lowercase letters are equivalent. The parameters you will see in this manual and some applications software manuals are explained in detail in Table App-1.

TABLE App-1 File Specification Parameters

[*filespec*]
The *file specification* is the complete description of the file, and may appear as [*filespec*] or as [*d:*][*filename*][*.ext*]

Examples: b:myfile.doc
a:yourfile
anyfile.bas
thisfile

An explanation of each part of the [*filespec*] follows.

[*d:*]
This parameter is the drive indicator. Enter the drive letter followed by a colon to indicate the intended drive.

For example, to obtain a directory of the disk in Drive B: (when B: is not the default drive), type **dir b:** followed by <CR>. The system displays the directory of the disk in Drive B:.

If you do not specify a drive in the command, the system assumes that the default drive is intended. For example, if the default drive is Drive A: and you type **dir** followed by <CR>, the system displays the directory of the disk in the A: drive.

[*filename*]
You may assign any name to a file as long as it meets the following criteria: The name assigned to the file can be from one to eight characters long; the only valid characters are A to Z 0 to 9 $ & @ % / \ _ - ( ) ' ` { } # !

Some versions of DOS and some applications software programs will not accept all of these characters. We recommend the use of the letters, numbers, and the _ (underscore) character for greatest compatibility.

[*.ext*]
The extension is optional for many situations, and pre-assigned by the applications software in other instances. The extension is from one to three characters long, preceded by a period, and follows immediately (no space) after the filename.

The characters listed above are the only valid characters. If an extension is assigned to the file (by you or by the software), it must be included as part of the [*filespec*] whenever you wish the system to locate the file.

THE DEFAULT DRIVE

The letter in the DOS prompt indicates the default drive. The default drive is the disk drive to which DOS will go automatically if you do not type a drive specification as part of a command or file name. On floppy disk systems, the default drive is usually A:; on hard disk systems the default drive is usually C:. Entering another drive letter will override the default. If you intend to perform a number of operations (Copy, Erase, Rename, etc.) on the files in the drive that is not the default, you may wish to change the default disk drive.

Changing the Default Drive

To change the default drive to B:, type

    A>b:<CR>   *The colon is required!*

To change the default drive to A:, type

    B>a:<CR>

To change the default drive to C:, type

    A>c:<CR>

The last command will not work unless you have a hard disk drive or a specially configured PC. Remember that the A> illustrated in the commands is supplied by the system, not typed by you.

PREPARING A DISK FOR USE

The FORMAT command is used to prepare a blank disk for use (a disk cannot be used to store programs or data until it is formatted) or to erase an entire disk which contains data you no longer need. The disk can then be reused. Unless you wish to use the FORMAT command to erase a disk, you need format each disk only once.

CAUTION: The FORMAT *command will effectively erase the entire contents of the disk.* If you have any doubts about the contents of the disk you are going to format, obtain a directory of the disk to insure that it does not contain any files you wish to keep (see the DIR command discussion in this appendix).

To Format a Disk

1. DOS should be loaded and the DOS disk should be in the default drive.

2. Type either

    A>format b:<CR>   *Floppy disk system; DOS disk in Drive A:.*

    C>format a:<CR>   *Hard disk system; DOS on hard disk which is Drive C:.*

```
A>format b:/v
Insert new diskette for drive B:
and strike any key when ready

Formatting...Format complete

Volume label (11 characters, ENTER for none)? steve ross


   362496 bytes total disk space
   362496 bytes available on disk

Format another (Y/N)?n
A>_
```

FIGURE App-2 Formatting a Disk with Volume Label
Note: Items entered by user are in **boldface.**

3. When the system prompts you to insert a new disk in the designated drive, make sure that the disk you wish to format is in the drive.

4. Press any key to begin the formatting process.

5. When the formatting process is complete, you will be asked if you wish to format another disk. If so, press the letter **Y** and follow the screen prompts to insert another disk. If you are finished formatting, press the letter **N**. Your data disk is now ready for use with the system.

Format with Volume Label

By using the /v option, you put an electronic label on your disk. When the DIR or CHKDSK commands are used, this electronic volume label will be displayed. The operation of the FORMAT/V command is illustrated in Figure App-2.

1. DOS should be loaded and the DOS disk should be in the default drive.

2. Type either

     A>**format b:/v<CR>**   *Floppy disk system; DOS disk in Drive A:.*

     C>**format a:/v<CR>**   *Hard disk system; DOS on hard disk which is Drive C:.*

3. When the system prompts you to insert a new disk in the designated drive, make sure that the disk you wish to format is in the drive.

4. Press any key to begin the formatting process.

5. When the system asks for the Volume label, enter any meaningful label, such as your name, identification number, or the contents of the disk. Use only legal file name characters. Press <CR> when the label is complete.

6. After the label is entered, you will be asked if you wish to format another disk. If so, press the letter Y and follow the screen prompts to insert another disk. If you are finished formatting, press the letter N. Your data disk is now ready for use with the system.

Bad Sectors

On occasion, the format process will report a number of bytes in *bad sectors* which means that the system was unable to format a portion of the disk. Often the problem is a speck of dirt, which will be dislodged if you try the format process once or twice more. If you receive a *bytes in bad sectors* message, answer Y to the *format another* prompt and leave the same disk in the drive. If the bad sectors persist after several tries, you should return the disk to where it was purchased and ask for a replacement.

THE DISK DIRECTORY

The directory, obtained by entering the DIR command, is a listing of the files on a specific disk. It is possible to display the directory of any disk on the system, and there are many variations of the command.

The Complete Directory

The DIR command, by itself, will display all files on the disk in the default disk drive. The [d:] parameter will yield the directory of the disk in a different drive. Examples:

   A>dir   *The directory of disk in drive A: (the default).*

   A>dir b: *The directory of disk in drive B:.*

   C>dir a: *The directory of disk in drive A: (hard disk system).*

An illustration of the use and result of the DIR command appears in Figure App-3. This command will tell you the disk volume label, how many files are on the disk, the size and date and time last modified of each, and the amount of space remaining on the disk.

Paused Directory

Once you have more than 20 files on a disk, you will not be able to see the entire directory on the screen at once. Use the /p option as illustrated in the following examples to cause the directory listing to pause after each screenful of information:

   A>dir/p
   A>dir b:/p
   C>dir a:/p

```
A>dir b:

 Volume in drive B is STEVE ROSS
 Directory of  B:\

KEYDOC11 DOC      3072    9-12-85     8:32a
KEYDOC2  DOC      2048    9-12-85     9:46a
FORMAT0  WKS      1536   10-20-85     9:27p
FORMAT1  WKS      1536   10-20-85     9:29p
EX1A     FW       1360    7-08-85     1:34p
EX1B     FW       7168    1-01-80    12:10a
SAMPLE_F FW      21952    9-16-85     1:21p
          7 File(s)     321536 bytes free

A>_
```

FIGURE App-3 Illustration of the DIR Command
Note: Command entered by user is in **boldface.**

Wide Directory

This form of the command produces a wide display of the directory, which lists only the file names and extensions, five across. Examples:

   A>**dir/w**
   A>**dir b:/w**
   C>**dir a:/w**

Printed Directory

The directory listing may be sent directly to the printer instead of to the screen by adding >**prn** after the command. Examples:

   A>**dir>prn**
   A>**dir b:>prn**
   C>**dir a:>prn**

DISK AND MEMORY STATUS REPORT

The CHKDSK command produces a disk and memory status report. The report will tell you how much space your files are using on the disk, how much space is available on the disk, and whether the disk has any bad sectors. This command will also indicate how much memory is installed and available in the computer system that you are using.

```
A>chkdsk b:
Volume STEVE ROSS   created Mar 22, 1986 12:43p


   362496 bytes total disk space
        0 bytes in 1 hidden files
    40960 bytes in 7 user files
   321536 bytes available on disk

   655360 bytes total memory
   453744 bytes free


A>_
```

FIGURE App-4 Illustration of the CHKDSK Command
Note: Command entered by user is in **boldface.**

1. The DOS disk should be in the default disk drive (normally drive A: on a floppy disk system, and normally drive C: on a hard disk system). If you want to check a disk *other* than the DOS disk, that disk must be in the other drive.

2. Type either

   A>**chkdsk**<CR>   *To check the DOS disk.*

   A>**chkdsk b:**<CR>   *To check the disk in the other disk drive.*

The result of the CHKDSK command is illustrated in Figure App-4. The *hidden file* is the volume label. The *bytes available on disk* refers to disk capacity. The *bytes free* refers to computer system capacity.

COPYING FILES

The COPY command allows you to transfer a copy of one or more files from one disk to another without erasing any of the data located on the disk to which you are copying, *except that a file from the source disk will overwrite a file with the same name on the target disk.* This is one method that may be used to backup data disks.

The disk that contains the files you wish to copy is called the *source disk.* The disk to which you are copying the files is called the *target* or *destination disk.*

In order to use this command, the target disk must be formatted and have sufficient bytes free (available) to hold the files being copied. The name of the file to be copied must be spelled correctly and include the complete *filespec* (drive designation if not the default drive, filename, and extension if present).

1. Place the source disk in one drive and the target disk in the other drive.

2. Type **copy**, a <SPACE>, enter the source drive, filename and extension next, another <SPACE>, then the target drive. Terminate the command with a <CR>. Consider the following examples.

   a. If the file you wish to copy is in Drive A: and the target disk is in Drive B:, you would type the command as follows:

      A>**copy a:filename.ext b:**<CR>

      Since a filename is not specified for the target (B:), the file on the target disk will have the same name and extension on both disks.

   b. If the file you wish to copy is in Drive B: and the target disk is in A:, the command would be

      A>**copy b:filename.ext a:newname.ext**<CR>

      In this case, the file on the disk in A: will have a different name and extension.

   c. To copy from the hard disk (C:) on a PC/XT or other hard disk computer, the command would be

      C>**copy c:filename.ext a:**<CR>

      As in case a., the filename does not change.

   With each of these forms of the command, you are specifying that you want to copy the named file from the disk in the first drive designated to the disk located in the second drive. Although you do not need to name the default drive, we recommend that you always name *both* drives to insure that the copy goes in the proper direction.

3. If the system cannot find the file, it will indicate *File not found* and *0 file(s) copied*. Check the spelling of the filename. Be sure you have included an extension if the source file contained an extension. If you have made a mistake, you may reenter the command.

Copy Using the Global Match Character

When you wish to copy several files which have file name or extension in common, use the global match character (*) to expedite the process.

1. Place the source disk in one drive and the target disk in the other drive.

2. Type **copy**, a <SPACE>, enter the source drive and filename next, another <SPACE>, then the target drive. Terminate the command with a <CR>. Consider the following examples.

a. If the file you wish to copy is in Drive A: and the target disk is in Drive B:, and the files to be copied have the same extension, you would type the command as follows:

   A>copy a:*.ext b:<CR>

   All files on the disk in the A: drive with the extension *.ext* will be copied to the disk in the B: drive. Neither filenames nor extensions will be changed.

b. If the file you wish to copy is in Drive B: and the target disk is in A:, and the files all have the same file name, the command would be

   A>copy b:filename.* a:<CR>

   All files on the disk in the B: drive with the name *filename* will be copied to the disk in A:. Neither filenames nor extensions will be changed.

c. To copy to the hard disk (C:) on a PC/XT or other hard disk computer, the command would be

   C>copy a:filename.* c:<CR>

   All files on the disk in the A: drive with the name *filename* will be copied to the hard disk (C:). Neither filenames nor extensions will be changed.

With each of these forms of the command, you are specifying that you want to copy the named file from the disk in the first drive designated to the disk located in the second drive. Although you do not need to name the default drive, we recommend that you always name *both* drives to insure that the copy goes in the proper direction. There are many additional uses of the global replacement character which are not illustrated here.

3. If the system cannot find any files which match, it will indicate *File not found* and *0 file(s) copied*. Check the spelling of the filename or extension. If you have made a mistake, you may reenter the command.

Copy All Files

With this version of the COPY command, you can copy all files from the source disk to the target disk. The target disk must be formatted and must have sufficient room for all the files. Files already on the target disk will not be erased, *except that a file from the source disk will overwrite a file with the same name on the target disk.*

1. Place the source disk in one drive and the target disk in the other drive.

2. Type **copy**, a <SPACE>, enter the source drive and *.* next, another <SPACE>, then the target drive. Terminate the command with a <CR>. Consider the following examples.

a. If the files you wish to copy are in Drive A: and the target disk is in Drive B:, you would type the command as follows:

    A>copy a:*.* b:<CR>

The files will have the same name and extension on both disks.

b. If the files you wish to copy are in Drive B: and the target disk is in A:, the command would be

    A>copy b:*.* a:<CR>

c. To copy to the hard disk (C:) on a PC/XT or other hard disk computer, the command would be

    C>copy a:*.* c:<CR>

With each of these forms of the command, you are specifying that you want to copy all the files from the disk in the first drive designated to the disk located in the second drive. Although you do not need to name the default drive, we recommend that you always name *both* drives to insure that the copy goes in the proper direction.

3. If the system cannot find any files, it will indicate *File not found* and *0 file(s) copied*. If you have made a mistake, you may reenter the command.

COPYING AN ENTIRE DISK

The DISKCOPY command is used to copy the entire contents of one disk to another. The target disk will be formatted if necessary. Be careful when you use this command, because anything on the target disk will be erased and unrecoverable.

1. The DOS disk or another disk with the DISKCOPY.COM program file must be in the default drive.

2. Enter one of the following commands

    A>diskcopy a: b:<CR>   *To copy from A: to B:*

    A>diskcopy b: a:<CR>   *To copy from B: to A:*

depending on which drive will hold the source diskette and which will hold the target diskette. Note: This command cannot be used to copy to or from a hard disk, but can be used on a hard disk system to copy from one floppy disk to another.

3. When the program has been loaded from the DOS diskette, you will be told to insert the source and target diskettes, and press any key when ready. Make sure you put the proper disk in each drive, then press any key to commence the disk copy process. You may make multiple disk copies if you wish.

DELETING OR ERASING FILES

Two commands, DEL and ERASE, are used to delete a specified file or files from the disk. The two commands are equivalent.

1. The disk with the file to be deleted must be in one of the drives (and you must know which drive).

2. Use the appropriate form of the command. Examples:

   A>del a:filename.ext<CR>   A>erase a:filename.ext<CR>
   A>del b:filename.ext<CR>   A>erase b:filename.ext<CR>
   C>del a:filename.ext<CR>   C>erase a:filename.ext<CR>

3. If the file is found and erased, there is no message. You can use the global character with these commands, just as with the COPY command, but be careful. Multiple file erasures are somewhat risky: it is easy to erase more than you intended.

4. If the system cannot find the file, an error message appears. Check the spelling of the file name and extension, and retype the command if you have made an error.

PAUSE DISPLAY

If information is moving on the screen or scrolling "off the top" of the screen too fast for you to read it, you may cause the display to pause until you are ready to continue.

1. Press the Ctrl key, then the Num Lock key, then release both. Output to the screen is suspended until you press any other character key.

2. Press any character key (including <CR> and <SPACE>) to resume display. You may use the Ctrl-Num Lock combination as often as you wish.

PRINT SCREEN FUNCTION

The print screen function is available through DOS and remains active in most applications programs. This capability is especially useful when you are having problems and no one is available to help you. Use the following procedure to make a screen print and take that print to your instructor or a friend for help.

1. Make sure the printer is turned on (usually there is a light indicating POWER) and on-line (look for an ON LINE indicator).

2. Press and hold <SHIFT>, press the PrtSc key, then release both keys.

3. The cursor traces the entire screen as the text is sent to the printer, then returns to its previous position when the system is ready for the next operation.

PRINTER ECHO FUNCTION

The print screen function is a snapshot: a view of the entire screen at a point in time. The printer echo function is more like a movie: once activated, everything typed or sent to the screen also appears on the printer until the echo is deactivated. Printer echo *does not* work with most applications software, and is generally used in DOS operations.

To Activate Printer Echo

1. Make sure the printer is turned on (usually there is a light indicating POWER) and on-line (look for an ON LINE indicator).

2. Press and hold the Ctrl key, press the PrtSc key, then release both keys.

3. Nothing will seem to have happened. Test the echo status by pressing <CR> once or twice. You should hear (and see) activity on the printer: the command prompt (A> or C>) is printed and the paper advances each time you press <CR>.

4. If you get no response in Step 3, repeat Step 2. You may have held the PrtSc key down too long, effectively activating and immediately deactivating the printer echo function.

To Deactivate Printer Echo

1. Press <CR> once to clear any text which has been sent to the printer.

2. Press and hold the Ctrl key, press the PrtSc key, then release both keys.

3. Nothing will seem to have happened. Test the echo status by pressing <CR> once or twice. You should not hear (nor see) activity on the printer.

4. If you get a response in Step 3, repeat Step 2. You may have held the PrtSc key down too long, effectively deactivating and immediately reactivating the printer echo function.

APPENDIX

 **THE WRITING PLAN**

INTRODUCTION

The key to clear writing is clear thinking. The writing plan described below will help you think and write clearly. You can then process your words with PC-Write and feel confident that those who read your document will understand what you have written.

THE WRITING PLAN

Your objective as a writer is to have the reader understand the content of the document you produce. If the reader understands your document, your writing is successful.

Helping readers understand your document requires clear thinking. Clear thinking is aided by a plan, or course of action. Here is a writing plan you will find easy to follow.

The steps in the writing plan are as follows:

1. Determine the purpose of the document

2. Prepare an outline

3. Gather facts

4. Write the document

5. Process the document

6. Correct the document

7. Submit the document

STEP 1   STATE THE PURPOSE OF THE DOCUMENT

Before you can promote understanding in others, you must first promote it in yourself. If the purpose of the document is clear in your mind, chances are it will be clear in the reader's mind.

A simple approach is to write out a one-sentence statement of your purpose. Here are some examples:

- The purpose of this letter is to provide information about our products' prices.

- The purpose of this memo is to summarize the results of our last sales meeting.

- The purpose of this term paper is to describe the educational backgrounds of the first three astronauts to land on the moon.

STEP 2   PREPARE AN OUTLINE

A good outline will help assure that your document a) has an understandable sequence of ideas, b) is not repetitious, and c) properly emphasizes important points.

Here is an example of a topic outline:

Introduction to PC-Write

I. Exploring an Existing Document

   A. Cursor control

   B. Cursor operating modes

II. Modifying Text in an Existing Document

   A. Adding text

   B. Deleting text

   C. Editing text

III. Saving a Document

   A. Saving and remaining in PC-Write

   B. Saving and quitting PC-Write

C. Saving with a different file name

IV. Printing a Document

The outline has four main ideas. Notice that the main ideas are separately and uniquely identified as I, II, III, and IV. Main ideas are separated from subordinate ideas (A, B, etc.) through identifying labels (either numbers or letters). Ideas of similar weight or importance carry similar identifiers. For example, the ideas represented by identifiers I, II, III, and IV are of equal logical importance in the outline. So are the ideas represented by the letters.

A topic outline should have at least two subdivisions. For example:

```
        A                               A
          1                               1
          2    is preferred,  not         2
        B
          1
          2


        A                               A
          1    is preferred,  not          1
          2                              B
        B
```

Where there is a I, there should be a II; where there is an A, there should be a B; where there is a 1, there should be a 2. The lack of a matching element usually means the thought is incomplete or the arrangement is illogical.

A topic outline is flexible. It can be made shorter or longer. You can extend the outline and emphasize each main idea with additional points, until you are satisfied that all important ideas are present and fully developed.

Thoughts can be arranged from different points of view. Common approaches to organizing thoughts are shown in Table B-1.

There is no one correct way to organize thoughts. The approach you take depends upon your subject. You are free to create any pattern you wish. Follow these guidelines when preparing a topic outline:

1. Group ideas (topic headings) based on their similarities or differences.

2. Arrange the topic headings according to main and subordinate relationships.

3. Identify each topic heading in a consistent fashion.

4. Use a combination of numbers and letters as identifiers.

TABLE B-1 Thought Patterns

I. Sequential Patterns (patterns in a prescribed order)

  A. Time-Related

    1. Recounting (traces events by date)
    2. Process (describes actions that lead to an end result; e.g., the steps in baking a cake, the steps in tuning an automobile engine)
    3. Cause and effect (describes relationship between some cause, such as smoking, and some effect, such as breathing problems)
    4. Problem-solving (details the steps necessary to resolve an unsettled situation)

  B. Space-Related

    1. Vertical/horizontal (relates material based upon up/down, near/far)
    2. Physical whole (relates material based upon systematic analysis of space relationships)

II. Hierarchical (ranking patterns)

  A. Deductive (thought progresses from whole to part; a generalization is stated and then supported by logically-deduced details)

  B. Inductive (thought progresses from part to whole; a detail is presented which is logically developed into a generalization)

  C. Abstractive (a broad statement or term is presented followed by material which clarifies the statement or defines the term)

III. Classification (organized relationship patterns)

  A. Similarity (material is grouped together because of similarities in type or category; specific arrangements can vary widely)

  B. Relationship (material is grouped together because, although separate and distinct, they all bear on the same subject; specific arrangements can vary widely)

  C. Importance (material is arranged by relative importance, as viewed by the writer)

STEP 3   GATHER FACTS

There are four ways to gather facts: a) by reading books, magazines, newspapers, and computer databases (called bibliographic research), b) by asking people questions, c) by observation, and d) by experiment. Fact-gathering for most document preparation usually involves methods 1 and 2.

Bibliographic research centers around library use. Use the card catalog (arranged by subject or author), or ask the librarian for help.

When interviewing people, write your questions down before the interview. In this manner you will obtain the information you want and not waste the other person's time.

When gathering facts, be sure you know whether you are dealing with a fact, an inference, or a judgment. A fact is something that can be proven true. An inference is something said about the unknown (it will snow this afternoon), based upon the known (it is snowing now). A judgment is an expression of opinion (I like snowy weather).

It is possible to arrange facts to distort a situation or to support a special interest. To minimize bias in your fact-gathering, a) gather information from different sources, b) use up-to-date sources, and c) accurately present what you find.

STEP 4   WRITE THE DOCUMENT

This step involves writing out your document, perhaps longhand. It comes after you have stated a purpose, prepared an outline, and begun to gather facts.

Your biggest task now is to write clear, mainly short (less than 20 words) sentences. A sentence represents a complete thought. Sentences are grouped into paragraphs.

A paragraph is a series of related sentences concerning one main idea. One of these sentences concerns the paragraph's main idea. It is called the "main" or "topic" sentence. It usually appears at the beginning of the paragraph. The remaining sentences support and develop the main idea.

If you copy material word-for-word from one of your bibliographic sources, make sure you surround the copied material with quotation marks (" "). It is acceptable to copy, or "quote." But you must inform your reader through use of quotation marks and you must cite your source. As a general rule, and especially for term papers, limit copying to about 20 percent of the paper. The rest should be your own words.

STEP 5   PROCESS THE DOCUMENT

You are now ready to transform your hand-written document into a business-like form. The result will be a document that is uniform in appearance, easily read, and suitable for reproduction. This may be done at a typewriter or a word processor.

We will use a word processor. A word processor is a computer with a special program in its memory. The program allows you to enter, correct, and print your document. The computer you will use is an International Business Machines (IBM) personal computer or a compatible machine. The program you will use is called PC-Write, an easy-to-use word processing software package. Once this program is loaded into the computer's memory, your document can be produced. The discussion on using PC-Write begins in Unit 2, The PC-Write Operating Environment.

STEP 6   CORRECT THE DOCUMENT

After you have printed your document for the first time, look it over and correct any obvious errors. Then put the document away. The next day, review your writing for clarity, spelling, and accurate statements of fact.

Try to show your document to someone else. Ask the person to mark the areas that are not clear or that contain errors. With changes in hand, return to the word processor and correct and print the document.

STEP 7   SUBMIT THE DOCUMENT

To be useful, a document must be available when needed. Submit or mail your document so that the reader may take timely advantage of what you have written.

REVIEW QUESTIONS

1. The most important person in written communication is

   _____

2. What is the main responsibility of a writer?

   _____

   _____

3. The seven steps in the writing plan are as follows:

   _____

   _____

   _____

   _____

   _____

   _____

   _____

4. You are about to prepare a document. How can you prove to yourself that you understand its purpose?

   _____

   _____

5. What is a topic outline?

   _____

   _____

6. What is the minimum number of subdivisions that should appear in a topic outline?

   _____

7. Identify the three main approaches to organizing thoughts.

_____

_____

_____

8. What are the four guidelines for preparing topic outlines?

_____

_____

_____

_____

9. Prepare a topic outline for each list of terms. Make up a suitable heading for each list. You can use the same term in your outline more than once. You may have to supply additional terms to make your outline logical.

List 1	List 2	List 3	List 4	List 5
adult	earth	head	hardware	marketing
female	wind	palm	user	manufacturing
child	fire	eyes	software	advertising
male		hands	stocks	
		ears		finance
		fingers		hiring

10. Here are some term paper subjects:

Space Travel	Car Repair
Techniques for Recording Music	The Family
The Three Branches of Government	Computers and Medicine
Drug Abuse	Television Watching
The Value of a College Education	The Home of the Future
Investing Money	Woman in Management
Selecting a College Major	John Dewey, Philosopher
The Writings of Charles Dickens	Guttenberg and His Press
Equal Opportunity	Sports in America
Major 20th-Century Events	Major Health Issues

a) Select any two and write a statement of purpose for each.

b) Prepare a topic outline for each subject you select. Develop at least four main ideas and carry the outline to at least a second degree of division.

c) Exchange outlines with another person. Evaluate each other's statement of purpose and outline.

11. How may facts be gathered?

_____

_____

_____

_____

12. Provide examples which show the difference between a) a fact and an inference, b) an inference and a judgment, c) a fact and a judgment

_____

_____

_____

_____

_____

13. What is a topic sentence?

_____

_____

14. Material that you copy from another source must be put in

_____

Use the appropriate format (see Appendix C) when answering the following questions. Use the writing plan described earlier in this unit.

15. Sales letters usually follow this pattern:

I Gain reader's attention.

II Provide facts about the product or service.

III Show how the product or service will benefit the reader.

IV Ask that the product or service be purchased.

Using this pattern, prepare individual one-page letters for any two of the following topics.

a. A line of sneakers.

b. The 1990 Moonbeam two-seat sports car.

c. A combination wrist watch, computer, sports car, and knife sharpener.

d. A audio-rack stereo system.

e. A condominium.

f. A magazine.

g. A candidate for political office.

h. A grass-cutting and lawn-care service.

i. A line of farm equipment.

j. A line of sports clothes.

k. A new microcomputer.

l. A travel agency.

m. A book on dieting.

n. A dating service.

o. Something you own.

p. Something you want.

16. Prepare a memorandum to your instructor which describes the elements of a word processor.

17. Prepare a report (maximum of six pages, double-spaced), on any one of the following topics.

    a. Any topic shown in question 10 above.

    b. Appendix A of this text.

    c. A hobby of yours.

    d. Your favorite college subject.

    e. The PC-Write <Esc>, <Alt>, <Shift>, and <Ctrl> main menus.

    f. Another word processing software package.

    g. A particular microcomputer brand or model.

    h. The last book you read.

    i. The first landing on the moon.

    j. A topic of interest to you.

18. Prepare a personal data sheet (resume) for a friend or relative. Gather the necessary information through an interview.

TYPICAL
DOCUMENTS

This appendix provides the typical formats for commonly used documents. Formats are provided for the letter, the memorandum, the term paper and the personal data sheet (resume).

THE LETTER

```
                    SOFTSIDE COMPUTERS
                      One Robin Lane
              Shelter Island, New York   11964
                      1-800-999-9999



                                    January 15, 1990



        Mr. Jeremiah Delacroix
        47 High Mountain Range
        Cloudscape, Colorado

        Dear Mr. Delacroix

        Here is the information you requested regarding the
        difference between a system disk and a data disk.

        A system disk (sometimes called a program disk) contains an
        application program.  The application program could be a
        word processing program, a spreadsheet program, a database
        program, or an integrated program.  An integrated program
        contains several application programs. In a dual drive
        system the system disk is usually placed in drive A.

        A data disk contains the files that are created through use
        of an application program.  For example, a word processing
        data disk stores the documents (i.e. letters, memorandums,
        and reports) created through use of the word processor.  A
        5 and 1/4-inch double-sided, double-density, floppy disk
        can hold a maximum of 112 data files.  In a dual floppy
        drive system, the data disk is usually placed in drive B.

        One last point.  Sometimes a disk which contains the Disk
        Operating System system files (the system files are those
        files necessary to bring the A> prompt to the screen) is
        referred to as a system disk.  So if someone hands you a
        "system" disk it could contain an application program, it
        could contain the DOS system files, or it could contain
        both.

                           Sincerely yours


                           Paul Smith
                           Technical Advisor
```

FIGURE C-1 THE LETTER (MODIFIED, OPEN BLOCK FORMAT)

THE MEMORANDUM

COMPUTER ANALYSIS ASSOCIATES

Interoffice Communication

TO: Oliver Flipback

FROM: Donald O. Sparta

DATE: June 24, 1990

SUBJECT: Formatting Floppy Disks With the PC-DOS /S Parameter

Here is the information you requested regarding the
formatting of disks using the PC-DOS /S parameter. If
you have further questions you can reach me at Extension
1956.

A disk formatted using the command FORMAT B: will prepare
that disk to accept program and/or data files. A disk
formatted with the command FORMAT B:/S directs the disk
operating system to also copy the DOS system files
(ibmbio.com and ibmdos.com) onto special disk tracks
called the system tracks. A third file, command.com, is
also copied to the disk. The ibmbio.com and ibmdos.com
files are hidden files. They are not listed on the
monitor when a DIRectory command is issued.

A disk containing the three files ibmbio.com, ibmdos.com,
and command.com, is capable of booting the computer. This
means the disk is capable of bringing the A> prompt to the
monitor. When the A> prompt is on the monitor, the user
can control the hardware and software. It does not matter
whether the files ibmbio.com, ibmdos.com, and command.com,
are placed on the application program system disk or on
the data disk. The three files can be placed on whichever
disk has available space.

If the ibmbio.com, ibmdos.com, and command.com files are
placed on the system disk, and the computer is booted, the
system disk can remain in drive A and the data disk can
remain in drive B. If the three files are placed on the
data disk, the data disk is first placed in drive A to
boot the computer. Once the computer is booted, the data
disk is removed from drive A and placed in drive B. The
program system disk is then placed is drive A.

FIGURE C-2 THE MEMORANDUM

The eight parts of Figure C-3 illustrate the format for a term paper report.

SLEEP AND ITS THRESHOLD

Cindy Lou Hoo

Queensborough Community College

October 23, 1990

FIGURE C-3 (Part 1) TITLE PAGE, TERM PAPER REPORT

TABLE OF CONTENTS

Page

2

FIGURE C-3 (PART 2)   TABLE OF CONTENTS PAGE, TERM PAPER REPORT

THEORIES OF SLEEP

Sleep Patterns

Almost every night every person living takes part in a mysterious function we call sleep. A third of an average person's lifetime is spent sleeping. This means we spend around twenty years almost immobile, remote from the waking world and rising and falling in waves of emotional experience we rarely remember.

The daily occurrence of sleep suggests that it has rhythmic importance to us. It appears that everyone is born with pre-set patterns. Because these forces are carefully scheduled, scientists call them "biological clocks". However, scientists have not yet been able to find out what makes these clocks work.

Why We Sleep

One of the biggest questions about sleep is: Why do we sleep? The first theory on

FIGURE C-3 (PART 3) DISCUSSION PAGE, TERM PAPER REPORT

4

record was set down by a Greek physician
named Alcmeon, who thought that sleep was
caused by the motion of the blood in the
veins. He thought that when a person got
sleepy his blood would flow out of his organs
and settle in pools in his veins. The person
would wake up when his blood flowed back into
his organs. Aristotle thought that since
people get tired after they eat that sleep
must be caused by the process of digestion.
Over the years scientists have proved that
these explanations are incorrect, no matter
how logical they may seem.

It is often thought that we sleep to
allow the body cells to eliminate wastes and
restore supplies of nutritional substances.
These sound like good reasons but they really
are not true. For instance, most of the
restorative processes of the body take place
during normal waking activity.

In Dr. Quentin R. Regestein's book,
Sound Sleep, he explains that one of the
reasons we sleep is that the cycle of
sleeping and waking conserves energy by

FIGURE C-3 (PART 4)   DISCUSSION PAGE, TERM PAPER REPORT

5

concentrating activity in a limited number
of hours. Another reason is that evolution
has equipped us to take care of the work of
survival during daylight. At night, we
conserve our resources so that they will be
available when we need to take care of our
life activities during the day. During the
caveman age, the people slept at night to
avoid natural enemies in the dark. Today
mostly everything at night is illuminated but
patterns established over hundreds of
thousands of years do not disappear quickly.
Therefore, we still sleep at night as the cavemen
did.

THE SLEEP OF LOWER ANIMALS

The experiences of lower species are
quite different than our experiences
concerning sleep. For example, the human
body's biological clock controls the body day
by day but some animals have biological
clocks that control activities that take
place just once a year. Fo instance, the
migration of birds and animals is timed by a
yearly clock. Another example of carefully

FIGURE C-3 (PART 5)   DISCUSSION PAGE, TERM PAPER REPORT

6

timed, once-a-year occurrences is
hibernation, the long winter sleep of some
animals. The ground squirrel gets ready for
winter by eating a lot in a short period of
time. The food he eats is then converted
into fat. When winter comes he crawls into
his den fat and sleepy. He emerges in the
spring thin and very hungry. Every part of
hibernation is dictated by biological clocks.
So it shows that the process of sleep by
lower species is quite different than higher
species.

THE THRESHOLD OF SLEEP

"The average sleep time is seven and
one-half hours, but anywhere between five and
ten hours is a normal night." <1>   A person
without sleep disorders will lie in bed
about fifteen minutes before falling asleep.
His body temperature starts to fall, muscles
relax, the amount of sugar carried in the

_____
1. Dianne Hales, "Twenty Eye Opening Facts
About Sleep,"(Seventeen, July, 1983), 42:108

FIGURE C-3 (PART 6) DISCUSSION PAGE, TERM PAPER REPORT

7

blood decreases and longer intervals are taken between breaths. He then gradually enters into a twilight zone as he becomes less aware of his physical surroundings. "Consciousness shifts from one subject to another, with progressively less logic and continuity." <2> During this first part of sleep th body is in a period of comfortable relaxation. A person may doze, then quickly awaken during this time and then doze again. The threshold of sleep is a very light sleep.

2. Quentin R. Regestein, M.D., Sound Sleep (Simon and Schuster, 1980), p.29.

FIGURE C-3 (PART 7)   DISCUSSION PAGE, TERM PAPER REPORT

8

BIBLIOGRAPHY

Hales, Dianne. "20 Eye Opening Facts About
    Sleep." _Seventeen_ 42 (July 1983): 108.

Regestein, Quentin R., M.D. _Sound Sleep_.
    New York: Simon and Schuster, 1980.

FIGURE C-3 (PART 8)   BIBLIOGRAPHY PAGE, TERM PAPER REPORT

THE PERSONAL DATA SHEET (RESUME)

Nna Amalak Anaroiam
1023 October Street
Shelter Island, New York   11964
615 947 8602

PRESENT CAREER OBJECTIVE

Eager to accept an entry-level position that will provide me with a training opportunity and the experience to assume account management position.

MAJOR QUALIFICATIONS

Knowledge of copy editing, page layout, marketing techniques, and related areas associated with an advertising agency.   A dependable self-starter with an outgoing personality.

EDUCATION

B.A. in English, cum laude, Dowling College, June 1987

HONORS

Kappa Delta Pi, National Education Honor Society
Sigma Tau Delta, National English Honor Society

ACTIVITIES

Secretary, Mu Tau Chapter of Sigma Tau Delta
Disc Jockey, Wing, Dowling College Radio Station

EXPERIENCE

Assistant Copy Editor, Ace Publishing, 50 Pelham Parkway, Bronx, New York, June 1985 - Present.

Sales Clerk and Advertising placer. Pastry for Your Tastry, 343 West 19th St., Dix Hills, New York, May 1984 - May 1985

REFERENCES

Mrs Rosalie Goldberg President, Ace Publishing 50 Pelham Parkway Bronx, New York 11002	Lauren Ann Sabella Manager, Baby Books Inc. 50 Campbell Lane East Islip, New York 11730
Arnold Krammer Professor, English Dowling College Oakdale, New York 11769	Barabara M. Dunne Owner, Pastry for Your Tastry 343 West 19th St. Dix Hills, New York 11730

FIGURE C-4 THE PERSONAL DATA SHEET (RESUME)

SELECTED
PC-WRITE MENUS

SYSTEM/HELP MENU

```
Esc F1:Help F2.Exit F3.Save F4.Command F5:Name F6:File F7:Print F8:Dir F9:Unsave
```

ESC MAIN MENU

```
F1:System/help    F3.Copy/mark    F5.Un-mark     F7.Paragraph     F9:Find-text
F2:Window/ruler    F4.Delete/mark  F6.Move/mark   F8.Lower/upper   F10:Replace
```

ALT MAIN MENU

```
aF1:Name/file     aF3:Key-record  aF5:Conversion  aF7.Pagebreaks   aF9:To-location
aF2:Spelling      aF4:Misc-stuff                  aF8.Upper-case   aF10:Replace-all
```

SHIFT MAIN MENU

```
sF1.Fn-keys-                                      sF7.Reform-      sF9:Location
sF2:Merging       sF4:Shareware                   sF8.Center
```

CTRL MAIN MENU

```
cF1:Ed-ED.dir     cF3.File-insert cF5.All-marked
cF4.Un-delete     cF6.Tofile/mark cF8.Right-flush  cF10:Swap=find
```

THE WINDOW (RULER LINE) MENU

```
Esc F1:Help F2.Clear F3:To-File F4.Insert F5.Default F6:From-file Grey- Col.nn
```

THE PRINT MENU

```
F1.Help-screen  F3.Finished     F5:Input-end    F7:Repeat-pages  F9.Page-stop
F2.Exit-to-DOS  F4.DOS-command  F6:User-input   F8:Skip-pages    D10.Continuous
```

PRINTING PC-WRITE DOCUMENTATION

The PC-Write program disk includes several files containing helpful documentation on the use of PC-Write.

To look at the documention on the screen, bring the DOS A> prompt to the screen, insert the program disk in drive A, and type TYPEMAN and press <Enter>. The documentation (approximately 60 pages) will appear one screen at a time with pauses so it can be read. To look at a particular page, specify how many pages to skip. For example, to look at page six, type TYPEMAN 5 and press <Enter>.

To print a copy of the documention bring the DOS A> prompt to the screen, insert the program disk in drive A, and type PRINTMAN and press <Enter>. The documentation (approximately 60 pages) will be printed. To print a particular page, specify how many pages to skip. For example, to print page six, type PRINTMAN 5 and press <Enter>.

To Interrupt viewing or printing, hold down <Ctrl> and press <Break>.

APPENDIX

SELECTED
PC-WRITE
MESSAGES

Some of the messages listed here may be slightly different from those in the program. See the
PC-Write manual for a complete list of messages.

EDIT PROGRAM MESSAGES

All Input file records merged, partial last record filled out
>   Merge finished; probably OK but check last Output document.

Cannot center or right-flush with current margins
>   A right margin must be set, and it must be greater than the left
>   margin.

Cannot create, maybe error in name, must cancel
>   DOS error trying to create name; probably error in file name.
>   Note: file names cannot contain a space and cannot exceed eight
>   characters.

Colon expected, Dot command ignored
>   Missing colon or another format error in this dot line.

Could not run print program
>   Could not find file PR.EXE, not enough memory, you are using DOS
>   1.x, or DOS error. Try changing the default drive by:
>   press <Alt>-F1, press F3, type A:, and press <Enter>. Then try
>   printing again.

Format incorrect
>   Merge document (input template) line has missing "}" or extra text
>   or other format error.

No marked or marking text

Copy, move, delete, and file copy need marked text to operate.

Not enough memory to show directory

The "memory" refers to the 60K limit on PC-Write files, not the size of your computer's memory. If you get this message it means your document file is at or near the 60K limit.

PRINT PROGRAM MESSAGES

Number expected

The value given for this dot line has the wrong format.

Text file line too long, extra ignored

A line in the input file is longer than 253 characters.

Too many footer lines

There are more than eight footer lines.

Too many header lines

There are more than eight header lines.

Will take user input lines when printing starts

The user input (F6) option will start after you press F9 or F10 to start.

Unknown second command letter

These two letters do not make a known dot line.

APPENDIX

G

THE SHAREWARE CONCEPT

(reprinted by permission of Quicksoft)

Quicksoft distributes PC-Write with a unique marketing approach we call **shareware**. The diskettes with all software and a short manual can be freely copied and shared with others, or purchased from Quicksoft for a small fee. We ask you to help us distribute PC-Write by sharing unmodified copies of the diskettes, to make it easy for other people to try PC-Write. We also permit unlimited copying of the diskettes to make it easy for people in a company, school, or other group to use PC-Write.

The term shareware includes copyrighted software, like PC-Write, which the author (Bob Wallace) supports and encourages people to copy and share, as well as public domain (non-copyrighted) software. Shareware is like public television: the programming is freely distributed, but support from users is encouraged. The concept is based on these principles:

- People need to try programs to see if they are useful.
- Software authors can be supported directly by users.
- Copying and networking of programs can be encouraged.

Quicksoft as a business depends on the sale of PC-Write manuals and support services to continue development of PC-Write and maintain our technical support and operations staff. If people who use PC-Write did not purchase these itms from us, we would go out of business. Fortunately for us, and for you as a user of PC-Write, a large percentage of users buy either the full PC-Write manual or a complete **registered** copy of PC-Write. Registration has a number of benefits:

- A hardbound copy of the full PC-Write manual.
- A PC-Write (Program) diskette with your unique registration number.
- Our PC-Write support service for one year:
  - Telephone (or mail) support for any questions.
  - A subscription to our quarterly newsletter, *Quicknotes*.
  - Creation of a printer control file for your printer.
- MS-PASCAL and assembly source files (not shareware)
- Thanks from us for your support and encouragement!

Your registration keeps us in business so we can enhance PC-Write with new features and operate in new environments and support you if you have technical problems or questions. We believe every user of PC-Write should have one of our manuals. Every user should also have our support service available, either directly from us, or indirectly through their organizations micro computer support staff who are supported by us.

Registered owners receive a commission when someone else registers from one of their copies. People who like PC-Write register and give copies to friends or associates with IBM PCs or compatibles. The commission is our way of thanking you for distributing PC-Write.

Quicksoft sells PC-Write and other materials in quantity. Larger organizations often copy the diskettes and buy our manuals. Registration for yearly support service is available separately if you already have a manual. Call or write for a full price list.

We really do encourage you to give away PC-Write diskettes, but there are some restrictions. As the copyright owner, Quicksoft permits you to sell or give away copies of the PC-Write (program and utility diskettes), with the following restrictions:

- You must distribute *all files* on the (program and utility diskettes) together.
- You must *not modify* any files except by using the Shareware Menu (Shf F4).
- You must *not* distribute copies of the printed manual.
- You must *not* distribute copies *outside the United States and Canada.*
- You must *not* distribute any files from the PC-Write source diskette(s).
- You *must* use *Quicksoft* copyright notices on media with Quicksoft files.
- You *must* use Quicksoft *trademark* notices on "PC-Write" and "Quicksoft"

You may add your own files, put files on several diskettes, distribute files via modem, or compress files as long as thrie contents remain unchanged. You may print, copy, and distribute the tutorial, the Quick Guide, or other text on the diskette. You need not notify Quicksoft when you distribute copies. Contact Quicksoft regarding licences to distribute modified software on a royalty basis, foreign translations, or other special cases.

INDEX

D

E

F

Notes

Notes

Notes

Notes

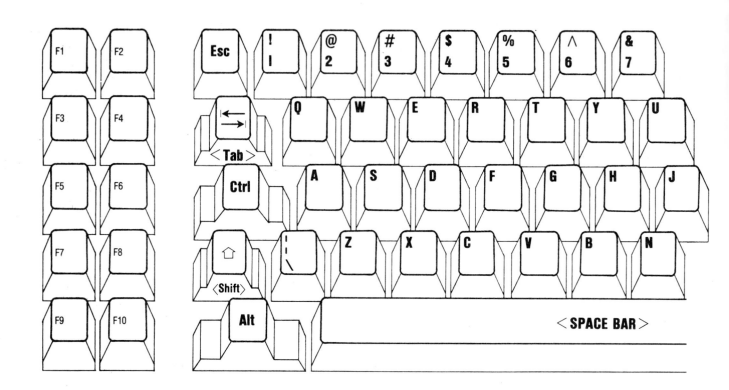

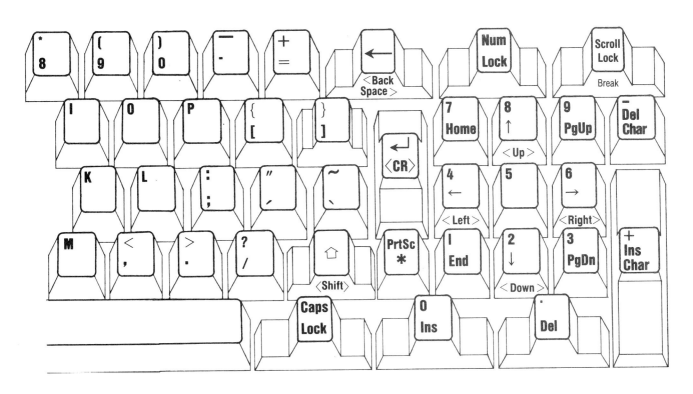

IBM PC™ Abbreviations

Esc—Escape Key

Ctrl—Control Key

Alt—Alternate Key

Num Lock—Number Lock Key

Pg Up—Page Up Key

PrtSc—Print Screen Key

Pg Dn—Page Down Key

Ins— Insert Character

Del— Delete Character

PC-Write

```
                          FONT CHARACTERS

 Key      Code  Char Font            Key      Code    Char Font
 Alt A    014   ♪    Align font      Alt M    007     •    Marine blue
 Alt B    002   •    Boldface        Alt N    017     ◄    Number font
 Alt C    006   ♠    Compressed      Alt O    019     ‼    Overstrike
 Alt D    016   ►    Double wide     Alt P    005     ♣    Pica
 Alt E    003   ♥    Elite           Alt Q    022     ▬    Quality
 Alt F    028   ∟    Fast            Alt R    030     ▲    Red
 Alt G    011   ♂    Guide line font Alt S    001     ☺    Second strike
 Alt H    024   ↑    Higher (superscript)  Alt T  012,15 ♀☼ Hard page break
 Alt I    021   §    Italics         Alt U    023     ↨    Underline
 Alt J    008   □    Jade green      Alt V    004     ♦    Variable
 Alt K    020   ¶    Keep paragraph font   Alt W  018     ↕    Double underline
 Alt L    025   ↓    Lower (subscript)     Alt Y  031     ▼    Yellow
```

MAIN MENU (Press Esc)

F1:System/help	F3.Copy/mark	F5.Un-mark	F7.Paragraph	F9:Find-text
F2:Window/ruler	F4.Delete/mark	F6.Move/mark	F8.Lower/upper	F10.Replace

F1:System/Help Menu

F1	F1	Help
F1	F2	Exit edit program
F1	F3	Save file
F1	F4	DOS shell
F1	F5	Change saving name
F1	F6	Switch files
F1	F7	Print a file
F1	F8	Directory
F1	F9	Stop save

F9:Find and Replace

F9	F9	Set Find text
F9	F10	Set Replace text

F2:Window/Ruler Menu:

F2	F2	Show/hide Ruler line
F2	F3	Append Ruler line to a file
F2	F4	Embed Ruler line into file
F2	F5	Read default Ruler line
F2	F6	Read Ruler line from file
F3.		Mark, copy marked text
F4.		Mark, delete marking text
F5.		Un-mark highlighted text
F6.		Mark, move marked text
F7.		Reformat para./marked text
F8.		Change case letter/marked
F10.		Replace found text

CTL MAIN MENU (Press Esc then Ctl)

cF1.Ed-ED-DIR	cF3.File-insert	cF5.All-marked		
	cF4.Un-delete	cF6.Tofile/mark	cF8.Right-flush	cF10.Swap-find

Ctl F1.	Load/update ED.DIR			
Ctl F3.	Insert file at cursor	Ctl F6.	Send marked text to file
Ctl F4.	Un-do last delete	Ctl F8.	Flush right line/marked text
Ctl F5.	Mark entire file	Ctl F10.	Swap "Find" w/ "Replace"

SHF MAIN MENU (Press Esc then Shf)

sF1.Fn-keys		sF7.Reform	sF9.Location
sF2:Merging	sF4:Shareware	sF8.Center	

Shf F1.	Display Main Menus on/off	

Shf F2:Merge Menu

Shf F2	F5	Edit merged Input record
Shf F2	F6	Stop merge
Shf F2	F7	Input merge record
Shf F2	F8	Output merge record
Shf F2	F9	Set merge file names
Shf F2	F10	Automatic repeat merge

Shf F4:Shareware Menu

Shf F4	F2	Change registration number
Shf F4	F3	Change front message
Shf F4	F4	Write changes to ED.EXE
Shf F4	F5	Quicksoft order form
Shf F7.		Automatic reform on/off
Shf F8.		Center line/marked text
Shf F9.		Show cursor location

```
ALT MAIN MENU  (Press Esc then Alt)
  aF1:Name/file    aF3:Key-record    aF5:Conversion    aF7:Pagebreaks    aF9:To-location
  aF2:Spelling     aF4:Misc-stuff                       aF8.Upper-case    aF10:Replace-all
```

Alt F1:Name/File Menu			Alt F3:Key-Record Menu		
Alt F1	F2	Set prefix	Alt F3	F2	Assign key
Alt F1	F3	Change logged drive	Alt F3	F3	Play back key sequence
Alt F1	F4	Change directory	Alt F3	F4	Turn Record mode on and off
Alt F1	F5	Rename a file on disk	Alt F3	F5	Define a key
Alt F1	F6	Copy entire file to disk	Alt F3	F6	Turn Numbers mode on and off
Alt F1	F7	Delete a file	Alt F3	F7	Unassign a recorded key
Alt F1	F8	Directory	**Alt F4:Misc-Stuff Menu**		
Alt F2:Spelling			Alt F4	F2	Insert Find text
Alt F2	F2	Check current word	Alt F4	F3	Word count
Alt F2	F3	Guess correct word	Alt F4	F4	Mark a pair
Alt F2	F4	Add word to list	Alt F4	F5	Insert current date
Alt F2	F5	Load user list	Alt F4	F6	To next non-ASCII character
Alt F2	F6	Save user list to disk	Alt F4	F7	Repeat last keystroke
Alt F2	F7	Turn on automatic checking	**Alt F5:Conversion**		
Alt F9:To-Location Menu			Alt F5	F2	Convert a Wordstar file
Alt F9	F7	Move to line x/x in file	Alt F5	F3	Convert dot commands
Alt F9	F8	Move to column x/x	Alt F5	F4	Convert tabs and spaces
Alt F9	F9	Move to line x/x on page	Alt F5	F5	Remove extra spaces
Alt F9	F10	Move to page x/x in file	Alt F5	F6	Fix line boundary errors
Alt F10:Replace-All Menu			Alt F5	F7	Remove page breaks
Alt F10	F9	Repeat replace	**Alt F7.**		Insert/display page breaks
Alt F10	F10	Un-replace	**Alt F8.**		Upper case letter/marked

EDITING COMMANDS	KEYS	CURSOR MOVES	KEYS
Delete		**Character**	
character at cursor	Del	left	Left Arrow
character to left	Bksp	right	Right Arrow
word to the left	Ctl Bksp	**Word**	
word to the right	Ctl Esc	previous	Ctl Left Arrow
line, from beginning	Shf Ctl Bksp	next	Ctl Right Arrow
line, from cursor to end	Ctl Enter	**Line**	
Insert		up one	Up Arrow
blank	Ins	down one	Down Arrow
line boundary	Enter	scroll up one	PgUp
Hard-Hyphen	Ctl Hyphen	scroll down one	PgDn
Soft-Hyphen	Shf Ctl Hyphen	beginning	Shf Home
Hard-Space	Ctl Space	end	End
Soft-Space	Shf Ctl Space	**Margin**	
Margins		to left	Home
temporary left margin	Ctl [	to right	Shf End
temporary para. margin	Ctl \	**Tab (or Margin)**	
temporary right margin	Ctl]	next	Tab
start new line, align		previous	Shf Tab
with text above	Shf Enter	**Sentence**	
Recording Keystrokes		next	Shf Ctl Right Arrow
Record mode on/off	Ctl @	previous	Shf Ctl Left Arrow
play back record	Grey*	**Paragraph**	
Slide Text		next	Ctl PgDn
to left	Shf Del	previous	Ctl PgUp
to right	Shf Ins	**Screen**	
Text Display		scroll one up	Shf PgUp
print screen	Shf Grey*	scroll one down	Shf PgDn
refresh screen	Ctl Grey*	**Screen Edge**	
Toggle		left	Shf Left Arrow
hide/show font chars.	Alt Space	right	Shf Right Arrow
Numbers mode on/off	Ctl ^	top	Shf Up Arrow
Pushright/Overwrite	Scroll Lock	bottom	Shf Down Arrow
Auto-reform/wordwrap	Shf F7	**Page Break**	
Transpose		next	Shf Ctl PgDn
character to the right	Shf Esc	previous	Shf Ctl PgUp
character to the left	Shf Bksp	**File**	
Hold Area		beginning	Shf Grey+/Alt +
mark, copy to Hold Area	Shf Ctl F6	end	Shf Grey-/Alt -
clear Hold Area	Shf Ctl F5		